Incredible Lessons Learnt as A Child

OrangeBooks Publication

Smriti Nagar, Bhilai, Chhattisgarh - 490020

Website:**www.orangebooks.in**

© Copyright, 2023, Author

First Edition, 2023

INCREDIBLE LESSONS LEARNT AS A CHILD

FOR CHILDREN AND ADOLESCENTS

CHARLENE HARRIOTT

OrangeBooks Publication

www.orangebooks.in

Content

Introduction .... *vii*

Acknowledgement ....**viii**

Nutrition.. **1**
  ❖ Thank you Lord for Your Blessings on Me

Exercise.. **9**
  ❖ Around the Walls of Jericho

Rest.. **15**
  ❖ Temple Made of Time

Water... **24**
  ❖ Little Feet be Careful

Sunlight... **30**
  ❖ Heavenly Sunshine

Temperance **37**
  ❖ Dare to be a Daniel

Air **45**
  ❖ Ezekiel Saw the Wheels

Trust in God... **51**
  ❖ Fill my Cup Let it Overflow with Love

Peace **56**
  ❖ Peacespeaker

Forgiveness... 62

   ❖ The Lord's Prayer

Love 66

   ❖ Love is something if you give it away

Faith 72

   ❖ Find us Faithful

Protection 77

Kindness 83

   ❖ Give and it will Come Back to You

Obedience.. 87

   ❖ Obedience is the Very Best

Disobedience.. 92

   ❖ Cooperation

Friendship 99

   ❖ My friend, do you Love Jesus?

Happiness.. 103

   ❖ Happiness is to know the Savior

Depression 108

   ❖ With Christ in the Vessel

Patience 114

   ❖ They That Wait Upon the Lord

Bibliography.. 119

Activities for Children 122

Introduction

In this book, you will find inspirational stories about children and adolescents experiences and how God inspired them. The topics are nutrition, exercise, water, sunlight, temperance, air, rest, trust in God, love, obedience, disobedience, friendship, kindness, faith, protection, happiness, depression, and patience. These topics will give wise counsel for daily living. It will uplift and bring hope and joy as you uncover the power of God in these stories. It has an activity section that you can use as well. Please enjoy exploring the pages of this precious children and adolescents book.

Acknowledgement

I want to thank the Almighty Father for giving me wisdom, knowledge, and inspiration to accomplish my goal. I want to thank my family and friends, especially my sister, for being supportive and standing in my corner. Reading this book will be a blessing to parents and their children. These inspiring stories will elevate, inspire and give wise counsel to children and adolescents.

Nutrition

One Sunday morning, when Joanne was nine years old, there was no food in the house. Her mother began attending the Seventh-day Adventist Church in Oregon, United States. The family migrated from South Korea, and her father decided he would never assist the family because the mother had accepted the Adventist faith. "If you choose God, let your God feed you; let your God clothe you," he stated. Her mother was unemployed, so she wept and prayed to God that Sunday morning in her room. When it was time for lunch, Joanne's younger sister grumbled, "I'm hungry." Her elder brother hid his expression, attempting to be courageous, although he could not assist. Joanne recalled reading in "Uncle Arthur's Bedtime Stories" about other children who prayed to God, and angels helped them.

"All we have to do is pray!" She shouted. "Uncle Arthur's Bedtime Stories says that if we pray, the angels will bring us food. Let's pray!" Her brother moved his eyes. Her younger sister lamented once again that she was experiencing hunger. Joanne never knew how to pray to God. "Hello God," Joanne stated. "We are hungry. 'Uncle Arthur's Bedtime Stories' says you can send us food, so would you send us something to eat, please?" They anxiously waited, but there was no food available for them. Several hours had passed by, and it was time for dinner. Joanne wondered, "What's wrong? God is late!"

The children became hungrier as time went by. Her mother continued to pray and cried to God in her bedroom. Finally, Joanne stated, "Oh, I know what we did wrong! God doesn't think we believe Him because we didn't set the table." She asked her little sister to go to the kitchen and get some metal chopsticks. The kids sat down after setting the table. "Sorry about that, God," Joanne said. "We probably did it wrong. Could you send us some food now? We're ready!"

But there was no response from God. The children went to bed dissatisfied and hungry that night. They awoke early in the morning to go to school. They had nothing for breakfast and no money to purchase lunch at school. "Don't bother, a large box full of food, Mother," Joanne said quietly. "She is still praying and crying." The kids opened the front entrance of the house to leave, but a large box full of food blocked their pathway. The children were surprised and summoned their mother to the door. Joanne was happy, and her mother was amazed at what she saw. Joanne was delighted that God had provided the food.

"The angels were just a little late!" She stated. Joanne realized that God is alive; he listens and responds to prayers. Joanne was convinced that the angels were Korean after the food miracle took place. "I tell you today that those angels are Korean," She stated. "The food that they delivered was all Korean. Everything you need to make rice, kimchi, and seaweed soup." Whenever you do not have anything to eat, pray in faith to God, and your prayer will be answered..

In 1947, the Namba Adventist Mission was placed in the hands of a native director after the white missionary left. There was no rain for a year, and the crops did not grow. The Mission was a long distance from any stores, and there was little money available to purchase food if it could obtain it. The mission director had been on an excursion to tour remote mission schools for some time. The Seventh-day Adventist believers in the central mission had depleted food supply and resources.

The wife of the native director gathered the families and informed them about the problem. She read the Lord's promises to the people and reminded them about the manna story that God had provided for His people during Moses' time, comforting them that God could send them food in the same way if they needed it. After prayer, her five-year-old daughter stepped out of the home and returned a short time later with her hands full of white substances eating. "What are you eating?" the mother inquired. "Out there, I saw six European men," the small one replied, "and they stated, the Lord has answered your request and has sent you manna; take it up and eat it."

The other people quickly rushed outside and discovered many acres of land coated with this white stuff. It was identical to the coriander-like seeds of the ancient manna. It had a wafer and honey taste to it. The people found no evidence of the Europeans when they went out to gather the manna. They assembled vast quantities of this nourishing manna, which kept them alive until they could find something else to eat. Angola went through a horrible period in which a civil war raged for more than two decades. During the civil war, the mission building was destroyed. After it was renovated in 2010, a vast portion of manna descended and covered the area. The manna now falls on Wednesdays and Fridays. When the church members are not in a good relationship with God, the manna that falls is bloody and bitter. The manna is white when the members are obeying God. God will always provide food for you once you ask him in faith.

Boys and girls should eat healthy foods to be strong and healthy. Here are different types of vegetarians. The major types of vegetarians are:

Lacto-Ovo vegetarians are persons who do not eat any meat or seafood. However, they eat dairy foods, like ice cream and cheese, and drink milk beverages. They also eat eggs and plant foods.

Lacto-vegetarians do not eat seafood, eggs, and meat; however, this diet includes plant foods and dairy products.

Ovo-vegetarians are people who do not eat seafood or dairy products but include eggs and plant foods.

Vegans or Total vegetarians are persons who only eat plant-based foods and avoid animal foods.

They are two other diets that are not strictly vegetarian but still focus on reducing the number of animal products eaten are:

Pescatarians do not eat meat but include seafood, dairy foods, eggs, and plant foods in their diet.

Flexitarians–people mainly have a plant-based diet that sometimes includes little portions of meat and seafood; sometimes also called 'semi-vegetarian.'

Sometimes as children, growing up as vegetarians eating lunch can be challenging. The best thing is to carry your meals to school, church, and trips. Children might look at you differently, or you might seem odd. Share the food with your friends and other students. Introduce them to healthy eating because it is a form of missionary work. Sometimes, if you cannot afford to prepare meals to carry for lunch, ensure you eat a healthy breakfast, a fruit for lunch, and a healthy dinner. When you start eating healthy as a child, as you grow older, you are less prone to certain diseases, and even if diagnosed with some health problems, you will recover more quickly. Growing up as a vegetarian can be challenging, especially when your friends eat meat; it can be very enticing. But pray and ask the Lord to assist you in maintaining your diet and not feel pressured to succumb to bad eating habits. Healthy eating is what God requires of us.

God, at creation, recommended human beings eat natural foods, such as seeds and nuts.

"And God said, Behold, I have given you every herb bearing seed, which is upon the face of all the earth, and every tree, in which is the fruit of a tree yielding seed; to you, it shall be for meat." Genesis 1:29. After Adam and Eve sinned, herbs were introduced into their diet. "And thou shall eat the herb of the field." Genesis 3:18.

When growing up, I never liked eating vegetables. However, I loved eating fruits. My mother insisted that I should eat vegetables. It was a challenge because they never tasted good to me, but later, I learned that we didn't eat for taste but for health purposes. Vegetables provide various vitamins and minerals that boost our immune system and act as antioxidants. Antioxidants are foods that help to fight against cancer and other diseases. Green leafy vegetables provide us with iron, which helps in the producing of red blood cells. Many children do not like to eat vegetables, which are good for their health.

Children and teenagers should follow healthful practices so that diseases can be prevented. Meals should be eaten three times a day and eventually, two times daily as they grow older. A plant-based diet should be practiced because God designed it from the beginning. Children and teens should learn that they eat to live and not live to eat. Children and adolescents should eat a balanced diet, including carbohydrates, protein, healthy fats, nuts, vitamins, and minerals. Eating the wrong food causes disobedience and frustration. But it is always wise to follow the diet that God planned for human beings. The foods that God gave us to eat are fruits and herb-bearing seeds. They will bring energy to the body. Fruits, nuts, legumes, vegetables, and grains are God's diet for humanity after sin. These types of foods, when prepared in a natural, simple way, are nutritious and healthy for the body. They give vitality, endurance, and a power of intellect that cannot be gained by a diet that is not healthy.

When you are a teenager, eating more nutritious foods is necessary for growing and maintaining health. Adolescents should ensure that they have healthy meals that provide energy. The adolescent diet should consist of essential nutrients such as protein, calcium, phosphorus, iron, zinc, and vitamins because of the rapid growth during this stage. Make sure that the diet includes green leafy vegetables and other foods that are rich in calcium. In addition, vitamin B12 and zinc supplements are recommended, especially during these teenage years, mainly if they are vegans. Children and adolescents should never eat unhealthy foods.

Children and teenagers should avoid eating fried foods like chicken, chips, doughnuts, and potato chips. These foods taste delicious, and the craving is there to eat more, but do not yield to the temptation. Avoid sweets like chocolate, ice cream, sweet biscuits, sweet drinks, sweets, and pastries. Try to eat baked or boiled foods instead. Eat fruits or vegetables instead of sweets and snacks. Children and adolescents should eat from different food groups, ensuring they are not deficient in nutrients. They should refrain from eating and drinking simultaneously during a meal. Instead, drink liquids at least an hour before meals or two hours after eating. Liquids interfere with the digestion process of food.

Eating too many sweets will increase the chance of tooth decay and type 2 diabetes. Some of these juices can be acidic, especially carbonated drinks. Toothaches can be painful; to avoid teeth decay, do not eat them so you can have pretty teeth and gums. Nobody likes to be smiling with decayed teeth or unable to eat some foods because their teeth are decayed. Acid destroys the enamel on your teeth that is there to protect them. You should protect the enamel on your teeth by drinking water instead. Start to eat healthy foods with your teeth so they can last longer. When the pancreas overworks results in a high amount of sugar in the blood, leading to diabetes. The stomach and the pancreas need rest to be able to function well. Make an effort to brush your teeth with fluoride toothpaste twice daily and for two minutes each time, and visit the dentist regularly to ensure your teeth are healthy. At creation, God ordained for everyone to eat healthy foods.

In creation week, God took six days to make heaven and earth. On the sixth day, he created man. "And the Lord formed man out of the dust from the ground, and breathed into his nostrils the breath of life, and man became a living soul." God made the Garden of Eden and put a man in there. Adam named the cattle, the fowl of the air, and all the animals. The Lord allowed a deep sleep to come upon Adam, and he removed one of his ribs and made Eve. He was happy that he had a companion and plants in the garden. Genesis 2. There was the tree of knowledge, good and evil, that they were not to eat from. Genesis 3:1-5. The Lord's plan for everyone is to eat natural foods. Fruits, grains, herbs, nuts, and vegetables will allow you to live a healthy life. Start eating healthy foods today, and you will never regret doing so. The Lord admonishes, "Beloved, I wish above all things that thou mayest prosper and be in health, even as thy soul prospereth" 3 John 2.

Thank you, Lord, for Your Blessings on Me

While the world looks upon me,

As I struggle along,

They say 'I've got nothing,

But they are so wrong.

In my heart, I'm rejoicing,

How I wish they could see.

Thank you, Lord,

For your blessing on me!

There's a roof up above me,

I've a good place to sleep,

There's food on my table,

And shoes on my feet.

You gave me your love, Lord,

And a fine family,

Thank you, Lord,

For your blessings on me!

I know I'm not wealthy,

These clothes, they're not new,

I don't have much money,

But Lord, I have you,

And that's all that matters,

Though the world may not see,

Thank you, Lord,

For your blessings on me!

There's a roof up above me,

I've a good place to sleep,

There's food on my table,

And shoes on my feet,

You gave me your love Lord,

And a fine family,

Thank you, Lord,

For all your blessings on me.

Exercise

Karen was about seven years old when a remarkable experience occurred at Avondale College in Australia. She was enrolled at this institution while her father pursued becoming a pastor. It was school sports day, and the day's last race had arrived. Unfortunately, it was also the longest race of the day; consider a group of seven-year-olds racing around a large field using chairs as markers. Any student who raced inside the seats would be disqualified, so observing and staying vigilant was critical.

Many girls about the same age lined up on the starting line for the race. Bang! They ran off as quickly as their legs would allow them to move. Some girls could run faster in the race than others because their legs were longer. Karen sprinted as fast as she could, passing one girl after another. She was approached by a group of girls running together, who invited her to join them. But she refused to do so. Karen passed them, but some girls were still in front of her at a distance from her.

Immediately, a loud voice shouted out from the sidelines, "Disqualified. You're out." "Oh no!" Karen said to herself. "I did not see that chair." She ran on the inside of the chair by accident. Would she give up at this moment? No way, she would never! After making a mistake, no dear child should ever give up. When we make a mistake, Jesus is always there to assist and forgive us of our sins. Keep this in mind! Karen made the decision never to give up and continued the race. She ran back to where she had started the race, around the chair until she was on the correct pathway. Almost all of the girls Karen had previously passed were now in front of her. She sprinted forward with each nerve and muscle in her body with determined effort. Karen kept her gaze straight ahead, not looking back. As she gazed forward, she noticed something unusual.

A tall distinct image of a man that Karen had not seen before stood well upfront. He was close to the finishing line, off to the side standing. Karen's eyes narrowed, looking at the figure as she quickly realized it was her beloved father. She couldn't remember him ever showing up at the school in such a manner as she noticed her father calmly watching her. A fresh surge of energy and thrill went through her body and thoughts. Karen passed almost all the girls on the field, running with weary legs and a painful side, gaze fixed on her father, and came to the finishing line in second place.

The most valuable present was the pleasant smile of her dad's acceptance. He wasn't a man who spoke much, so that smile meant more to her than the apple she got for her valiant efforts. She knew her father was happy because she persevered in the race. "Wherefore seeing we also are compassed about with so great a cloud of witnesses, let us lay aside every weight, and the sin which doth so easily beset us, and let us run with patience the race that is set before us, Looking unto Jesus, the author and finisher of our faith; who for the joy that was set before him, endured the cross, despising the shame, and is set down at the right hand of the throne of God." Hebrews 12:1-2.

Children and teenagers should always be physically active for at least 60 minutes during the day. Aerobic activities allow you to move all the big muscles of the body. Some of these exercises are: swimming, running, playing tennis, and walking briskly. In addition, there are exercises that you can do that permit flexibility. They make you extend your body and tighten the muscles of your body. These exercises enhance good posture, strengthen muscles and bones, decrease stiff muscles and improve relaxation. These exercises include digging in the dirt while gardening, digging in the sand at the beach, climbing the stairs, and raking leaves. Another type of exercise you can do is strengthening. It strengthens the muscles, bones, improves posture, and assists you in growing and developing. Some activities include climbing the stairs, raking the leaves, and doing sit-ups and push-ups. They must engage in physical activities that will enhance the development of the brain and will provide an exciting learning experience for them.

Children and adolescents should always participate in household chores for both boys and girls. If they do not do any activities, their bodies will become weak because human beings are made to move. Those who are physically disabled and cannot move should also do appropriate exercises, such as isometric exercise (squeezing the body tightly). Children who are disabled should exercise the limbs that they can move and those they cannot move. They should not only stay indoors and play games, read and do schoolwork. Children and adolescents must go outside in the fresh air and exercise every day if they can do so. If they have to stay indoors, let them exercise inside. Children and adolescents should not stand idling; they should always be active in doing something worthwhile. They should never be burdened with other activities and not be physically active. If children practice being physically active from early on, they will continue this healthful practice in later years. Instead of doing evil deeds, they ought to do good work. It prevents them from being overweight and improves lung function, which aids in the exchange of air so the heart can circulate oxygenated blood, allowing your skin to be pink and beautiful. Other benefits of exercise are improved self-confidence, a healthier heart, friendship and social interaction with other people, enjoyment in learning new experiences, improved concentration, and focus in the classroom.

As we enjoy participating in physical activities daily, we should exercise our faith and trust in God. We are to believe that he will answer our prayers according to his divine will when we pray to God. When we cannot solve our problems, we should walk in faith. "For we walk by faith, not by sight." 2 Corinthians 5:7.

When the Israelites were going around the walls of Jericho, they had to walk in faith.

Jericho was closed, and no one could gain entry or exit from the city. Therefore, all the men of war should go about the city once, which should be for six days. Joshua told the people they should not make any noise until he told them. The seven priests should bear seven trumpets of ram's horn before the ark, and on the seventh day, they should march around the city seven times, and the priest would blow the trumpets. When they made a loud blast with the ram's horn and heard the trumpet sound, everyone would shout with a great voice; the city wall would fall flat to the ground, and the people would enter the city.

The seven priests blow the trumpet for six days. The children of Israel marched around the city on the seventh day, blowing their trumpets. Joshua told them to shout for the Lord had given them the city. Everybody shouted with a great shout, and when the priest blew the trumpets the wall fell flat. Everyone went into the city, and they took the city. Joshua 6: 1-27.

The Christian life is a race that all faithful children of God can win. Nobody will ever be disappointed at the end of the Christian race. The strongest and weakest athletes in the Christian race can win the race through determination, sincerity, and persevering faith in God. Everyone can win the Christian race through God's amazing grace once they have totally committed their lives to him. The Christian race is not for the strongest or the weakest athlete; the one who endures hardships and exercises a persevering faith in Jesus will win the eternal crown. Children and teenagers, for you to win the Christian race, ask God to help you overcome sinful behaviors. Only athletes with a pure Christian character will win the prize of eternal life.

The athlete must practice self-discipline to win a race, so the Christian athlete can be disciplined to win the Christian race by following God's Ten Commandments and listening to the Holy Spirit. As the child of God grows in the knowledge of God and develops a closer relationship with him, the individual with determined effort and zeal will be victorious in the Christian race.

Keep your mind focused on God daily, run the Christian race with patience, and never give up. Ask God to give you patience, strength, and faith to run the Christian race. Whatever challenges you face, continue to run the Christian race and never stop running, even if you feel like stopping; God will give you a golden crown. "And let us run with patience the race that is set before us." Hebrews 12:1. "Know ye not that they which run in a race run all, but one receiveth the prize? So run, that ye may obtain. Now they do it to obtain a corruptible crown, but we an incorruptible." 1 Corinthians 9:24- 25.

When you go through this life being a faithful servant running the Christian race, you will say at the end of it, "I have fought a good fight, I have finished my course, I have kept the faith: Henceforth, there is laid up for me a crown of righteousness, which the Lord, the righteous judge, shall give me on that day: and not to me only, but unto all them also that love his appearing." 2 Timothy 4: 7-8.

Around the Walls of Jericho

Around the walls of Jericho,

Around the walls of Jericho,

Around the walls of Jericho,

The army went.

Seven times without a stop,

Seven times without a stop,

Seven times without a stop,

The army went.

When the people gave a SHOUT,

When the people gave a SHOUT,

When the people gave a SHOUT!!!

The walls fell down.

So, into Jericho at last,

Into Jericho at last,

Into Jericho at last,

The army went.

Rest

Luis got an unexpected holiday when all the public schools in Peru closed. The teachers went on strike for two months because they wanted the government to give them better salaries. When Luis' school reopened, the teacher warned the students that they would have to work harder to make up for the two months. Saturday was added each week as an extra day of class. On Saturday, Luis did not want to study. Subsequently, after attending a Vacation Bible School in his hometown of Cusco, he surrendered his heart to Jesus and was baptized earlier that year.

The teacher informed the students that they should remember to come to school the other day because they had an essential examination. Luis approached the teacher cautiously after the last class on a Friday. He explained to her, "I am a Seventh-day Adventist. Please allow me to take the exam another day because I go to church on Saturdays." The teacher thought for a moment. However, Luis had always received good grades, so he hoped the teacher would accept his decision. When Luis returned home, he informed his parents about the problem, although they were not Seventh-Day Adventists. "It depends on the teacher," Mother said. "If the teacher gives permission, then you can skip school on Saturdays, but if she doesn't, you must go to school." Luis prayed before going to sleep that night.

"Help me and make the teacher give me permission," he prayed. "Sabbath is a holy day set aside by you, and I have to worship on this day." However, the teacher and his parents did not permit Luis to attend church on the Sabbath. Luis still attended church. He never spoke to anyone at church about his challenge. He felt humiliated, but he continued to pray that God would persuade the teacher to permit him not to go to classes on Saturdays. Luis was anxious when he came to school at 7 am on Monday. He never wanted to talk to the teacher about his problem. All day, the teacher did not speak to him about the situation. Finally, the teacher ordered him to the front of the classroom as the other students left for the day. He went to the teacher, trembling. The teacher gave a kind smile, "It's OK," she said. "Your grades are good. I'll let you make up for Saturday school work on other days of the week."

He was overjoyed because God had heard his prayers. Luis ran home as swiftly as he could to inform his parents about the good news with a bright smile. Luis prayed before going to sleep that night, "Thank You for helping me get permission to go to church on Sabbaths." When he woke up that morning, he praised God again. Luis is now hoping that something else that seems unthinkable after such a beautiful answer to his prayers, his parents will be baptized in the Seventh Day Adventists church. "If God could answer my prayer about not going to school on Sabbath, then I am sure that he will answer your prayer," Luis stated. A great blessing awaits those children who keep the Sabbath holy.

Another miraculous story of faithfulness in keeping the Sabbath is about Ruzala.

Ruzala sat in church listening to the soul-stirring sermon of her pastor as she battled in her mind to take away her thoughts from the test that she missed in school that Sabbath. She refrained from breaking the Sabbath, even if she never graduated with her class. Instead, she placed her situation in God's care, knowing he would solve her case. Ruzala did not realize that her decision to serve God and keep the Sabbath day holy would have spared her life. Azerbaijan [ah-zehr-bai-jahin] is the country where Ruzala lives. There are few Christians in her home country. Ruzala's father was a Christian, but he was not happy with the church he was going to and sought a church that taught Bible truths.

When she was thirteen years old, she recalled visiting her grandmother when she saw people coming out of a church close to her home. She informed her father about the church and encouraged him to visit it. As a result, her father inquired from their neighbors about the Seventh Day Adventist Church close to her grandmother's home.

He discovered it was a Seventh-Day Adventists church. These church members were called the "believers". Dad decided to attend the church to learn about their teachings. He was happy to associate with these Bible-believing Christians. The other family members were invited to attend church with him two weeks later. The children attended church with their father, but their mother was hesitant for many months before she decided to attend church with her family. Finally, the children and their father were baptized together. When Ruzala attended high school, it was challenging to be steadfast in her Christian beliefs. Not many Seventh-Day Adventists are in her country, and few people know the beliefs.

Some teachers pressured Ruzala and her sister to refrain from going to school on Saturdays. As a result, her sister was expelled because she refused to attend classes and do her examinations on Sabbaths. Ruzala anticipated the same fate as her sister. She was not expelled, but her teachers gave her poor grades because she missed classes and examinations on Saturdays.

Ruzala prayed to God each day for assistance to pass her examinations without breaking the Sabbath. She received blessings from God because of her faithfulness to him. Her final examination schedule was posted as graduation approached closer, but one was planned for Saturday. I will not go, she said to herself. Ruzala prayed, "Dear God, help me to honor your Sabbath and still graduate." When she attended church on Sabbath, it was difficult to concentrate on the preaching. As the minister was about to announce the closing hymn, an explosion smashed the air, it shook the windows and the people inside the church. In the distance, a siren moaned. The congregants were ushered outside the church when the worship service was over. Ruzala noticed smoke that seemed to be coming from the school she attended. Afterwards, she saw some of her classmates and rushed to inquire about what had occurred.

"There was an explosion at the school!" A girl stated. "Someone said that the military teacher brought a hand grenade to school and left it in his classroom while students were taking their test. Someone started playing with the hand grenade, and the safety pin came out. The grenade exploded, and lots of kids got hurt! I think one boy even died!" Her heartbeat was heavy, as she recognized that if she had attended the school that day, she would be inside the classroom where the explosion occurred. She rushed to the school to find out for herself what had happened. She started to cry when Ruzala saw a hole in her classroom building resulting from the grenade that exploded. The students that were wounded received treatment and were placed in ambulances.

Ruzala believed that it was the Sabbath that saved her life. She said her life was saved because she refrained from attending Saturday classes. One teacher saw her and told

Ruzala, "You were lucky not to be here today," the teacher stated. "Your faith has saved you." "Yes," Ruzala responded. "My faith and my God saved me." Many of her classmates assembled around her. Some of the students asked her questions about her faith in God before. However, they saw how Ruzala's God had shielded her from the incident on that particular day. The students explained their appreciation that her God was there with her. Although the parents of the students prohibited them from attending a Christian church, her friends know that her belief is in the hands of a caring and compassionate God. Her faithfulness in keeping the Sabbath was an incredible witness to God. This story reminds us to keep the Sabbath holy.

"Remember the Sabbath day, to keep it holy. Six days shalt thou labour, and do all thy work: But the seventh day is the Sabbath of the Lord thy God: in it, thou shalt not do any work, thou, nor thy son, nor thy daughter, thy manservant, nor thy maidservant, nor thy cattle, nor thy stranger that is within thy gates. For in six days the Lord made heaven and earth, the sea, and all that in them is, and rested the seventh day: wherefore the Lord blessed the Sabbath day, and hollowed it." Exodus 20:8-11.

Whenever Friday comes, it is the preparation day for the Sabbath. As a child, I was responsible for cleaning everyone's shoes in the family. So everyone would be a part of the preparation. We baked and cooked for the Sabbath day.

We complained that the Friday night worship services at home were too boring. We suggested to our parents how we think the worship should be conducted. In addition to the hymns, we sang, we had lively choruses, a special song, a testimony, repeated scripture verses from memory, and we also said the Ten Commandments from memory. It was a pleasure for us because we were in charge. When our parents were in charge, we had so many complaints. We even said it was too long. But when conducting the services, we never cared if it was long. In the evenings, our parents would study the lesson for our age group. We also had our regular morning and evening worship. The evenings were spent with each other telling how their day was. Everyone in the family, whether the child or the parent, would encourage each other.

On Sabbath, we would eat what was prepared on Friday. It was an enjoyable day because we did nothing but eat and go to church. If we never go to church, we would conduct our services. We would have Sabbath School as a church. I was the superintendent, and my Brother did the lesson study. My sister would do the special song, and my parents were the congregation. They would have to say, praise the Lord, hallelujah, amen, just as what occurred in the church. If they did not do this, we would not be pleased. They had to be obedient to us, and they would comply.

In divine service, we sang the hymns, and the preacher prayed. The other activities were: offertory, Bible reading, pastoral prayer, and special song. Then the sermon would be preached by my brother, and the rest of the family sat and listened attentively.

The Sabbath is a delight and should be enjoyed and not be burdensome. Children and teenagers should not play games on the Sabbath at all, whether at home or church. Only Christian-related information should be watched on the Sabbath. They should participate in missionary activities by giving out Christian literature, caring for the elderly, singing, reading the Bible and Christian books, and helping the less fortunate. Children and teenagers should have personal devotional activities such as prayer, reading the Bible, and Christian stories, listening to gospel music, and doing bible quizzes. They should also participate in church activities during the week and on Sabbaths, whether at church or online. Children and adolescents should participate in Bible studies at home, the Bible class at church, and underline Bible verses that mean something to them. Write and meditate upon the word of God.

Children and teenagers can do online ministries using social media platforms like WhatsApp and youtube, sending godly messages and videos. In addition, communicating with other people online by sharing encouraging messages and sermons encouraging each other in the faith are ways that children and teenagers can minister to their peers and adults.

Children and teenagers can do nature walk on Sabbaths and during the week. Nature teaches about the love of God, for instance, the colors, variety of shapes and sizes of trees and flowers.

They can listen to the melodies of the breeze, the swaying of the trees, and the songbirds chirping. As they continue to walk, they can smell the odor of pine trees, examine the lovely green grass, and the perfume of flowers. Children and adolescents can touch the texture of tree bark and the leaves tenderness on plants moist with rain. When they have a completed look at the flowers, plants, and birds, they should state how many types have been identified, smelled, and touched. They should enjoy learning about God on the Sabbath day. Make your time useful, learning about God in the early years of life. When you grow older, it will be a pleasure to teach others; to live a Christ-like life and avoid doing evil deeds of the enemy.

Jesus loves when boys and girls do things that honor him. He will give them abundant blessings. But if you spend time doing evil practices, it will not be pleasing in the eyes of God, and you will suffer from your actions. If you do the right, you will have struggles, but God will always help you through these challenges. But if you engage in sinful practices, you will be repaid with these deeds and more. Christ kept the Sabbath holy; children and teenagers should follow his example. "And he came to Nazareth, where he had been brought up: and, as his custom was, he went into the synagogue on the Sabbath day and stood up for to read." Luke 4:16.

When Jesus died for our sins, he rested in the grave on the Sabbath day, and he rose to life on Sunday, the first day of the week. Matthew 28, Mark 16, and Luke 24.

The Sabbath is a beautiful day for rest.

Children and adolescents also require physical rest. When you do your activities, always remember to take a break. If you are studying, no matter how small the activity is, take a break from what you are doing. After doing physical activities, take a break. Rest energizes the body to always have the strength to do other activities. Always participate in activities at home, church, or community. Don't spend time idling; always try to do something to occupy your mind. There should be a balance in the activities you do, study God's word and academic work, play with other children, and rest.

The rest times for children are: infants that are under one year old should have 12-16 hours; children 1-2 years old should have 11-14 hours ; 3-5 years old 10-13 hours; 6-12 years old at least 9-12 hours and adolescents 13-18 years old 8-10 hours. Sleep is one of the essential components of a healthy lifestyle and integral to everyone's daily pattern. It assists in the growth and development of your body. According to studies, children and teenagers who get enough sleep regularly have a better attention span, memory, learning, behavior, and mental and physical health. Conversely, inadequate sleep can result in high blood pressure, irritability, obesity and depression.

While Jesus lived on earth, he would rest from his labors. On one occasion, when his disciples were sailing on a boat, he fell asleep, and his disciples woke him to calm a storm, and he did. Luke 8:24. Jesus and his disciples took time to rest when they finished their duties for the day. They would move away from the people and rest for a while. "And he said unto them, Come ye yourselves apart into a desert place, and rest a while." Mark 6:31. He also would spend time praying alone to his heavenly Father in a mountain or in a quiet place. "And in the morning, rising up a great while before day, he went out, and departed to a solitary place, and there prayed." Mark 1:35. "And when he had sent the multitudes away, he went up into a mountain apart to pray: and when the evening came, he was there alone." Matthew 14:23.

In the Bible, there are many stories on rest; one is about a young man named Eutychus. Many lights were in the upper chamber where they had all gathered. Eutychus sat in a window. He fell into a deep sleep while Paul was preaching, and Eutychus fell from the third loft. He was dead, so Paul went down and fell on him and embraced him. Paul told the people that life was in him. They brought the young man alive. God spared the life of the young man. Acts 20:7-12. Although physical rest is important, mental and spiritual rest are also significant. Whatever your struggle is, do not worry and never bear it on your own. Give it to Jesus and tell him how you are feeling. Talk to Jesus like, just as how you would talk to your parents or friends. He listens to children and teenagers as well. The Lord says, "Come unto me, all ye that labor and are heavy laden, and I will give you rest. Take my yoke upon you, and learn of me; for I am meek and lowly in heart: and ye shall find rest unto your souls. For my yoke is easy, and my burden is light." Matthew 11: 28-30. Children should spend time in prayer, reading the Bible and other spiritual books as these activities will build their mental and spiritual health. They will be able to cope with life's challenges because Jesus is their true friend.

Children and teenagers should not worry about their problems and should not be anxious about anything or try to solve difficulties on their own. Never murmur, complain about your problems and carry a sad face; it will make you ill.

Carry your problems to Jesus; he will solve them and give you the strength to cope. "Casting all your care upon him; for He careth for you." 1 Peter 5:7. "Cast thy burden upon the Lord, and he shall sustain thee: he shall never suffer the righteous to be moved." Psalm 55:22.

Exercise your faith in God by praying to him about your problems, for he understands and cares about you. At times you will experience pain and the loss of a loved one, and you feel you cannot bear it anymore; remember that Jesus loves you dearly. Just rest your mind on Jesus by thinking about his goodness towards you.

Temple Made of Time

God took six days and created the earth and moon; the stars and sun.

On the seventh day, He rested from the work that he had done.

Then He blessed it, made it holy as a gift for every man.

To remind us where we came from and just how this world began.

Chorus

Holy day purified, set apart, sanctified.

Enter into joy divine, in a temple made of time.

See Him worship on the Sabbath as His weekly custom was.

Feel the fury of the rabbis, for He would not heed their laws.

So they killed Him on a hillside as the sun began to fade.

But He even kept the Sabbath as they laid Him in the grave.

Oft forsaken and forgotten, desecrated and profaned.

But the sacred commandment is still valid and unchanged.

Hear the Father gently calling, "If you love me, heed each one,

Not for merit or salvation, but because you love my son."

Water

Cibele lived in the remote community of Piraí along the Amazon River, which is situated in Brazil. Apart from going to school, she mainly stayed at home. The other children of the village had mocked her ever since she was a child whenever she left her house. "You are strange," a girl smirked. After her father's leg was crippled in a boat accident, he could not work, and because of this, the children teased Cibele. "Oh, there goes the daughter of that hopeless man who can't work," a boy stated.

When Cibele was seventeen, she heard a knocking at her door one day. She saw young ladies greeting her with a huge embrace upon opening the door. She was surprised because she had never seen those ladies before. However, she enjoyed the hugs. "Hi, we are missionaries from the Seventh-day Adventist Church," one young woman said. "What's your name?" After speaking with her, the two missionaries went to another home.

The following day, the missionaries came back to talk more. They told Cibele on the third day that the boat church Amazonia de Esperanca (Hope Amazon) had come and invited them to attend the boat church's evangelistic meetings. Naturally, Cibele wished to attend the boat church, although she always liked staying home. "I'll go!" She exclaimed.

Cibele persuaded her parents to follow her to the meetings. Cibele and her mother brought Dad from their home to the boat church. Pastor Reno preached about Christ and lived on the boat church. While the pastor was preaching, she recognized that Jesus Christ would love to have a close connection with her. She thought of her father, who couldn't walk for fifteen years, and believed Jesus also cared for him. Each day she prayed for his healing. "Thou visitest the earth, and waterest it: thou greatly enrichest it with the river of God, which is full of water: thou preparest them corn when thou hast so provided for it. Thou waterest the ridges thereof abundantly: thou settlest the furrows thereof: thou makest it soft with showers: thou blessest the springing thereof." Psalm 65: 9, 10.

The father of Cibele captured her attention at a boat meeting and asked for assistance to walk to the bathroom two weeks later. Halfway to the bathroom, he uttered, "Let me try to go just a short distance on my own." Cibele observed her dad taking a few steps. Finally, Cibele's father went to the bathroom, and both returned to the boat church meeting hall. The pastor paused preaching, and people looked in astonishment. "It's a miracle!" exclaimed Cibele, in tears "It is God's miracle!" From that day, Cibele's classmates began to treat her respectfully, and they started attending the sessions. "We have never heard anything like this before!" They told her. A month later, after the meetings started, Cibele was baptized with her parents, sister, and cousin. Water was used to baptize Cibele's father, which was utilized spiritually. However, water is used physically as well.

The island I live in, Jamaica, is surrounded by water. We have seas, rivers, springs, and ponds. Water is all around us, and we also use water from the pipes to care for our personal needs. However, only some see it necessary to drink water or drink the amount we should. This is because the human body comprises 75% water and the earth's surface. Humans might live without eating food for six weeks; however, no one can survive without water for more than a week because we were made to be continuously moistened.

Water is essential to the movement of nutrients to cells and the removal of toxins (poison from the body) for excretion. Water is lost through urine, sweat, breath, and feces. The older you get, the more water your body loses, depending on the age. The amount of water you have lost in your body should be replaced. For example, a girl 9-13 years-old, will lose about 1.4 liters of liquid through urine, sweating, breathing, or feces. The quantity of water also depends on the atmospheric temperature, and your health, and some health conditions limit your fluid intake, like kidney disease. This amount of water should be taken even more, especially if you participate in activities involving great energy and generating sweat. Water keeps the mucus membranes moist, lungs, mouth, nose, eyelids, digestive system, urinary system (tract), and vagina. It controls body temperature, assists digestion, and decreases the risk of constipation. In addition, it prevents the skin from being dry. Children and teenagers are more easily dehydrated than adults. Because most of their body is made up of water and the metabolic rate is higher, they are more active than adults.

Dehydration means there is a deficiency of water in the body. Some symptoms include cracked lips or dryness, high body temperature, skin might be bluish, weakness and tiredness. Some of the causes include inadequate drinking of water, diabetes, heat, diarrhea, vomiting, and fever. In addition, children are prone to gastroenteritis, an inflammation of the stomach and the intestine. This involves mainly diarrhea and vomiting. Coconut water, if available, is beneficial to treat dehydration because it provides the body with liquid and nutrients.

We can receive water from soya milk and almond milk, non-caffeine teas, sugar-free juices, like fruit juices but not too much, vegetable juices, purified water, and coconut water. Children and teenagers should avoid sugary drinks and drink purified water when tempted. They should also avoid caffeinated teas, coffee, alcoholic and carbonated beverages. Ensure the water you drink has fluoride in it. It helps with the protection of the enamel of the teeth. The enamel is the hard outer section of the teeth.

Children and teenagers should drink water throughout the day, especially in a hot climate. Always carry water when going to school, church, or doing outdoor activities. Water will hinder you from getting dehydrated and keep you well hydrated. You should drink purified water and avoid contaminated water from rivers, ponds and springs. If you have to drink water from these sources, boil it before drinking. Apart from drinking, water is used for many other purposes. An essential purpose that water is used for is hygiene.

Ensure proper hygienic practices are maintained at all times. Hand washing is necessary to be done: before and after eating, after using the restroom, before and after consuming fruits, before and after having a meal, before preparing a simple meal, and touching dirty surfaces. Fruits, vegetables, and ground provisions must be washed before preparing. Hand washing helps prevent many diseases; children and teenagers should always practice proper hand washing. If water and soap are not available to wash hands, use hand sanitizer or alcohol to rub your hands.

Ensure you have a daily bath. Younger children should bathe more regularly than older children and teenagers. Children and teenagers should bathe at least twice during the day. Bathing helps to cleanse and refresh both body and mind. Warm and cool baths assist in blood circulation throughout the body and calm the nerves. A cold bath helps in reducing the effects of a fever. Cold, cool and warm baths are great remedies for the body. Water helps in the prevention and curing of many diseases. Cold water also helps to relieve pain and reduces excessive bleeding. Water has a significant role in our lives.

Plants, animals, and the environment cannot function without water. Water quenches the thirst of animals and human beings. When we don't have rainfall, there is drought, and people suffer. Despite how scarce water is, we cannot live without it; whether in health or illness, purified water is one of the greatest blessings God has given to human beings. Jesus Christ is the water of our lives. No matter your age, you should thirst after knowing Christ, the water source. As the animal desire water, we should go to Christ. "As the hart panteth after the water brooks, so panteth my soul after thee, O God." Psalm 42:1. Jesus Christ himself used water to wash his disciples' feet.

Before the Passover feast, Jesus knew that his hour had come and he should depart this world and return to his Father that had sent him into the world. The enemy had placed in the heart of Judas to betray Jesus. Jesus left the supper, laid aside his garments, and took a towel. He placed water into a basin. He washed his disciples' feet and wiped them with the towel that he took. Peter told Jesus that he should never wash his feet, but Jesus told him he would not deal with him. Peter then said he should wash his hands and head also. Jesus knew that Judas would betray him that day; he said you were not all clean. Jesus washed all their feet and told them they should wash each other's feet. If they practice doing these things, they would be happy. John 13:1-17. If we drink from his fountain, we will never be thirsty again.

The true water source is Jesus, and he calls us to drink from his fountain. "And he said unto me, It is done. I am Alpha and Omega, the beginning and the end. I will give unto him that is athirst of the fountain of the water of life freely." Revelation 21: 6. When we read the word of God, he speaks to us. When children and teenagers read God's word, pray and do what God wants them to do, they drink from the fountain of life. As we have a closer relationship with Jesus, we will be like him.

Little Feet, be Careful

I washed my hands this morning,

So very clean and white,

And lent them both to Jesus,

To work for Him till night.

Refrain:

Little feet, be careful,

Where you take me to;

Anything for Jesus,

Only let me do.

I told my ears to listen,

Quite closely all day through,

For any act of kindness

Such little hands can do.

My eyes are set to watch them,

About their work or play,

To keep them out of mischief

For Jesus' sake all day.

To keep them out of mischief,

For Jesus' sake all day.

Sunlight

The father of Mary was the manager of a lighthouse on the British coast. The lamps shone in the night to help navigate the ships and provided protection from dangerous shoals and rocks. The lighthouse appears to say, "Take care, sailors, for rocks and sands are here. Keep a good lookout and mind how you sail, or you will be lost." Mary was the only person in the lighthouse one afternoon. Her father had trimmed the lamps to light when evening arrived. He needed to purchase food, so he crossed the bridge which led to the land. The bridge was a pathway that was over sand and rocks. It was utilized for two or three hours each day. During other periods the waters arose and encircled the bridge. Mary's father wanted to hurry home before the water covered the bridge. The night was approaching, and a storm was developing on the sea. The waves struck the rocks, and the wailing wind encircled the tower.

Her mother had died, and she was by herself; her dad informed her that she should not be scared because he would return home soon. Some suspicious men were at the back of the rock, and they were observing the father of Mary. The men watched him while he was going on land. Who were these men? These men were "wreckers" that loitered around the coast. When a vessel was drifting on the rocks because of a storm, the men hurried to the ship, not to assist but to steal from the people and ransack the ship.

These cruel men knew that a small girl was alone in the lighthouse. So they organized for her father to stay on the shore for the entire night. The ships were filled with rich cargo and were supposed to sail towards the point before dawn. The men knew the vessels would move upon the rocks and be ruined if no light shone. How devious and heartless these men were for their intention to kill the ship's crews.

He had filled his basket and was ready to return to the lighthouse. When Mary's father came closer to the road leading to the bridge, the pirates hurried from hiding and attacked him. The men tossed him to the ground. The pirates swiftly tied his hands and feet with ropes and brought him into a hut. He had to remain there until dawn. He cried out helplessly for them to release him. These cruel men only ridiculed his suffering. Afterwards, they left two men to oversee him while the others returned, dashing to the shore.

"Oh, Mary, what will you do?" Moaned father as he lay in the hut. "There will be no one to light the lamps. Ships may be wrecked, and sailors may be lost." The little girl observed from a small window towards the shore. She was wondering if her father would come back in time. Mary was aware whenever it reached six o'clock, the water would cover the bridge. One hour had passed, it was seven o'clock, and she looked at facing the beach, but her dad was not in sight. Finally, at eight o'clock, the water was almost covering the bridge. Only tiny pieces of rocks were seen on top of the water. "Oh, father, hurry," Mary moaned as if her dad was listening to her. "Have you forgotten your little girl?" The only reply came from the loud sounds of the sea waters moving higher and higher. As the roaring wind blew, Mary realized that a storm was approaching. There would be no lights coming from the lamps that night.

Mary was thinking about what her mother usually uttered: "We should pray in every time of need." So swiftly, she knelt and prayed to God for his assistance "O Lord, show me what to do, and bless my father, and bring him home safe." Now the water was flowing over the bridge. Sunset had taken place over an hour before, and the moon appeared; stormy black clouds were seen encircling it. The pirates moved along the shore and watched for other ships to land on the coast. They wished the sailors would not see any lights and would believe that they were far away at sea. During this time, Mary decided to attempt to light the lamps. What could Mary do since she was such a small girl? Mary decided that she would try to light the lamps at this time.

The lamps were far beyond her reach. She took matches and brought a tiny step ladder to the location. She discovered that the lamps were over her head. Mary took a little table and put the step ladder on top of it. She realized that the lamps were still above her head when she did that. "If I had a stick," she stated, "I would tie a match to it, and then I could set alight to the wicks." But she found no stick. The raging storm was nearly like a hurricane. The sailors watched along the seacoast for any light and wondered where the lights were. Did they sail in the wrong path? The sailors were lost at sea and were unaware of where to steer the vessel.

During this time, her father prayed to God to care for his precious little girl in the lonely and unlit lighthouse. Mary was scared because she was all alone; she would sit down another time. Then, a thought came to her mind that an old book was in a room below her. The book was precious to her because it was her mother's own. So she inquired, "Wouldn't she allow me to take it if Mother was here?" At that time, she carried the huge book and put it below the ladder's steps, and she climbed another time. Mary reached the lamps, so she lit each one until bright lights shone from them way above the dark sea waters.

As her Dad lay in the hut, he saw a bright light and praised God for answering his prayer in this time of danger. Sailors saw the bright lights and moved the ships from the rocky paths. The pirates also saw the lights and were angry because their evil plans had failed. Throughout the stormy night, the bright rays of the lamps shone over the raging sea. When dawn approached, her father ran away from the hut. As he arrived at the lighthouse, he discovered how his little girl demonstrated faithfulness to the task during the stormy night. Jesus is the world's light; we cannot live without him.

We cannot live without sunshine because we would cease to exist. Most plants thrive more with exposure to sun rays than those exposed to artificial light. People exposed to the sun's rays daily are healthier, and their complexions are more beautiful. However, exposure to sunlight is important, but too much can cause dehydration, sunstroke, and skin cancers. If you're not exposed to sunlight or limited sunlight, take a supplement of Vitamin D.

Vitamins in food are unlocked by the sun. We wouldn't get the most out of our meals if it weren't for the sun's rays. The process known as photosynthesis is the method plants use the sun's beams to extract carbon dioxide and oxygen from the atmosphere and combine them into the essential food substances that all life depends on. Chlorophyll is the green component in plant leaves; photosynthesis is responsible for this. It is incomprehensible because it is the marvelous work of God. One of the most powerful agents for natural healing is sunshine. Sunlight keeps our blood warm and pure while providing life-giving energy to all organs. Our brains are nourished by sunlight-enriched blood, and the sun's energy strengthens our bodies. For example, cholesterol is a type of fat that is produced by the body, and it is used for different functions. The sun changes cholesterol into vitamin D, which decreases blood cholesterol levels. Vitamin D has many health benefits, including allowing the calcium to work better in the body, helping with bone development, which assists in the prevention of bone diseases like rickets in children and osteomalacia in teenagers, tooth decay, creates stronger bones, speeds up wound healing, and relieves other health conditions.

Sunlight is the best natural and most powerful disinfectant that helps to get rid of germs and builds the immune system, which fights against germs in your body. Windows should be opened to allow sunlight in the home. Sunlight relaxes your mind and body. It aids in brain function, helps to relieve sadness, makes your heart stronger and makes the blood flows better in the body. It helps to prevent lung disease, and sleep is improved by exposure to sunlight, especially at night. The sun's healing qualities are highly beneficial to the sick. Sunlight enhances liver function, aids waste disposal, and is an excellent treatment for jaundice. It relieves part of the strain on the kidneys by allowing wastes to pass through the skin when you sweat. Sunlight is vital for children to grow healthy. Children should play in the sunlight. They should admire nature for its beauty in the sunshine. They should sing praises to God in the sunshine along with the birds.

King Hezekiah was ill to the point of death. Isaiah told him that he should make his house orderly because he would not recover. Hezekiah moved his face toward the wall and prayed for God to help him. He told the Lord that he walked faithfully with his whole heart and had done well; he wept bitterly. Isaiah was in the court when the Lord came to him and told him that God had heard Hezekiah's prayer, saw his tears and would heal him. God gave him fifteen years to live. After that, he would deliver the city from the Assyrian king. Isaiah prepared a fig poultice and placed it on the sore that Hezekiah asked Isaiah for a sign that he would be healed. He gave Hezekiah a message that God would bring the shadow of the degrees, which went down in the sundial of Ahaz. Ten degrees backwards so the sun turned light ten degrees. 2 Kings 20: 1-11 and Isaiah 38. God used the sun as a sign of healing for King Hezekiah. "Truly the light is sweet, and a pleasant thing it is for the eyes to behold the sun." Ecclesiastes 11:7.

The sun is also used to identify the time and the seasons of the year. The instruments that are used to determine time relating to the sun include the sundial and the sun stick. The sundial is the most ancient instrument used to identify the time of the day. The time was known by how a shadow was positioned due to the exposure to the sun's rays. The shadow changes its position whenever the sun's rays move, hence determining the time of day. The sundial was used to mark the movement of the sun. As the day continues, the sun rotates across the sky, causing the shadow to move, thus indicating the course of time.

A stick is placed in the ground, and the tip of the shadow caused by the stick is marked. Whenever the shadow decreases, it's noon (12 pm), and when the time past noon, the size of the shadow increases. The sun usually rises in the East and sets in the West. Therefore you can identify the time of the day by where the sun locates. Whenever the earth faces the sunlight, it is morning (sunrise); when the earth moves away from the sun, it is evening (sunset). When the earth rotates on its axis and moves around the sun, sunlight penetrates the earth at various angles, which causes shadows. Marking the areas where the shadows fall, you will count the number of times they move; this activity shows time.

Whenever the earth moves nearer to the sun, it is summer, and the climate is warm. The climate is cold when the earth moves further from the sun; this is winter. In countries, closer to the equator, the distance from the sun doesn't change, so the year's season remains the same.

"The sun shall be no more thy light by day; neither for brightness shall the moon give light unto thee: but the Lord shall be unto thee an everlasting light, and thy God thy glory." Isaiah 60:19. Jesus is the sunshine of our lives.

It is so important to have exposure to sunlight, and it is also essential to let your light shine for Jesus. Share the sunshine of Jesus' love with your friends, family, and community. You can share a scripture, invite them to church, give them a tract, Sabbath school quarterly, and a book. Encourage them to join a club at a church, sing, share a meal, and share clothes , but the best way to be a light for Jesus is to be a living example. You can do this by following the life of Jesus and the commandments of God, being obedient, and honest. "Let your light so shine before men, that they may see your good works, and glorify your father, which is in heaven." Matthew 5:16. Children should enjoy the sunshine of God's love.

Heavenly Sunshine

Heavenly sunshine, heavenly sunshine,

flooding my soul with Glory divine,

Heavenly Sunshine, heavenly sunshine,

hallelujah, Jesus is mine.

How are you, neighbor? How are you, neighbor?

So glad to see you shake hands with pleasure.

How are you, neighbor? How are you, neighbor?

So glad to see you, please come again.

Temperance

An unfortunate young man named Alean went to a prestigious school one morning and requested to see the principal at the door. An employee observed his tattered clothing and thought he looked like a beggar. He was informed to go to the kitchen. He followed the employee's instructions and soon emerged at the back door of the building. "I would like to see Mr. Brown," he asked. "You want a breakfast, more like," the employee said, "And I can give you that without troubling him." "Thank you," the boy answered, "I should have no objection to a bit of bread, but I should like to see Mr. Brown if he can see me."

"Some old clothes, maybe what you want," the employee asked, looking at the boy's patched pants. "I guess he has none to spare; he gives away a lot," without paying attention to the boy's request, the employee placed some food on the kitchen table and continued her task. "Can I see Mr. Brown?" He inquired again after completing his meal. "Well, he's in the library. Of course, if he must be disturbed, he must, but he does like to be alone sometimes," responded the employee in an irritable voice. She seemed to believe it was unwise to let such an unappealing young man inside her employer's office. But, on the other hand, she cleaned her hands and beckoned for him to follow her.

On opening the library door, she stated: "Here's somebody, sir, who is dreadfully anxious to see you, and so I let him in." She was unaware of how the young man presented himself or the way he opened his business; however, she is aware that after talking for some time, her boss, the principal, laid down the book he was researching, picked up some Greek books he had in the library and started to assess the young man. The assessment lasted for a while. Each question the principal posed, the boy responded eagerly. "Upon my word," cried the principal, "You certainly do well!" Then, looking at the boy from head to foot, over his glasses, he inquired, "Why, my boy, where did you pick up so much?" "In my spare moments," the boy replied.

He was impoverished but industrious and had few chances for schooling, but he was almost ready for college by using his spare time wisely. Aren't spare moments truly the "gold dust of time"? What a priceless treasure they would be! What kind of account can you produce in your leisure time? What proof do you have for them? Take a look. The young man informed you of the benefits of using your spare time wisely. Several boys and girls are incarcerated in the bar or where you play pool. If they were asked how they started their sinful practices, they might reply, "In my spare moments."

"In my spare moments, I played addictive games."

"In my spare moments, I began to smoke and drink."

"It was in my spare moments that I began to steal candy from the corner store."

"It was in my spare moments that I gathered with wicked associates." Children should be cautious about how they use their leisure time. Often time temptations occur in these free times. The Devil will attempt to get into your heart in these spare times. He will conceal himself and organize mischievous actions. Therefore, children should use their leisure time wisely with the help of God. "But I keep under my body, and bring it into subjection: lest that by any means, when I have preached to others, I myself should be a castaway." 1 Corinthians 9:27.

Temperance is the balance of doing good and the absence of doing evil.

My father would prepare our meals when my mother was not around as a child. When he gave us our dinner, he provided us with a lot of food. I sometimes remember when we were through, we could not stand up. We had to wait for some time, and even when we waited, we would eat again, trying to finish the food, but we could not. When we even think we could get up and walk. We were unable to move for a while. We ate just too much food.

When we overeat food, we will gain weight. The blood providing the necessities for the body, particularly the brain, will be redirected to the stomach instead and stay there longer than usual.

Drowsiness will occur after consuming a large portion of a meal. It also leads to becoming tired and not being able to think clearly. Temperance would prevent this situation.

 Another form of intemperance is a sexual relationship before marriage. Having early sexual intercourse initiates a link with a risk of having multiple lifetime sexual partners, unprotected sex, acquiring sexually transmitted infections (STIs), and unwanted pregnancy. Do not engage in sexual practices until you are married. Abstain from it because it is for adults, not for children or teenagers. It will prevent early pregnancy and teenage pregnancy. I remembered my friend Catherine (pseudonym); we were children. She became pregnant at the age of twelve years old. It was so devastating to her family. Her mother was devastated, and the people who supported her stopped assisting her. It affected her schooling because she had to attend another school. She never completed her high school education.

If you have urges to have sexual intercourse because it starts at different ages, pray and ask the Lord to control your feelings. Engage in activities in your community, school or a church. Participate in activities that help your development, like caring for the elders, visiting children's homes, and other activities. Exercise also controls sexual desires. Read the Bible and spiritual books in your free time. Do not idle your time and keep your mind occupied all time. Try to do constructive activities, and be cautious of the type of music you choose to listen to because it will evoke sexual feelings. Be careful of what you watch on the television, internet and social media. If the music does not honor and glorify God, do not listen to it. If your activities do not glorify God, do not participate in them. Keep friends that will help in your development to live a pure life. Do not be close to children or teenagers who will influence you to do evil deeds.

Do not stay in the company of older women and men alone in an enclosed area, for example, at home, church, or school; if you don't know them or trust them, it could be a family friend or a family member. If they try to molest or molest you, do not hesitate to tell your parents, parent, or guardian. If you cannot approach your parents or they refuse to listen, talk to a school teacher, guidance counselor, or police officer, or if you are unsure, pray to the Lord to direct you to the right person to tell. Do not keep it a secret; speak if you are threatened. Pray and read the word of God because the Lord can protect and support you.

Never allow anyone to touch you inappropriately to make you feel uncomfortable. The main areas of the body that are untouchable include genitals (penis or vagina), buttocks, breasts, abdomen, and thighs; never allow anyone to touch them; it doesn't matter who the person is. Never allow anyone to feel you all over your body or force you to sit on their lap, even if it's a parent or a family member. Children and teenagers should never allow anyone to be too familiar with them, especially adults or older teens. They should never allow anyone to bribe them with money or other things for sexual pleasure; children and adolescents should be satisfied with what their parents give them. Finally, children and adolescents should have respect for God and themselves.

Children and adolescents are precious jewels in God's sights therefore, they are not to allow anyone to sexually abused them; they should seek help and never allow fear to silence their voices. You are a precious property of God, not for sale. Children and teenagers should avoid having close friendships with strangers on social media platforms or offline. They should also be observant of the behaviors of family members and family friends towards them. Whenever they feel uncomfortable around a family member or family friend, they should avoid them. When you start to engage in sexual practices, you are prone to have sexually transmitted diseases like human immunodeficiency virus (HIV), gonorrhea, syphilis, and herpes. Some might become teen fathers and mothers, which can be very burdensome to you and your family.

Pray and let the Lord control you. Try to have a good friendship with both sexes without not having sexual or intimate intentions. Dress modestly by wearing clothing that limits exposure to your body. Never forget that your body is God's temple. Engaging in sexual practices can be emotionally destructive because you are not mature to handle the effects of this emotional behavior. Early sexual exposure can also cause cervical cancer and emotional scars for life. Children and teenagers should never visit people's homes without parental consent; they should never travel alone but ask someone to accompany them. Children and teenagers should travel in groups, a boy and a girl should not travel alone, especially if they are not related. Trust God. He will guide you through your steps.

Another form of intemperance is drug abuse which children and adolescents must avoid. Avoid using all forms of drugs by not smoking or using them in any form, such as ganja, cocaine, crack tobacco, heroin, ecstasy, and foods containing them. Alcoholic beverages mean all drinks and food that contain them should also be avoided. When you use drugs, it tempts you to do criminal activities. Children and teenagers should avoid committing crimes using weapons like knives, guns, sharp instruments, stealing, and other sinful practices. Do not hurt yourself or be pressured into your friends' wrongdoing. Walk away from fights and conflicts. Live at peace with everyone.

When you practice these sinful behaviors, you will also not be able to complete school, and you can be a burden to your family and friends because your practices are unacceptable. You will not appreciate a healthy lifestyle that prepares you for this life and eternal life. Your memory will be impaired, and you will not be able to remember as you should, especially when you are on drugs because it damages your brain. You will have mental health problems and even mental illness. Many children and teenagers become mentally ill because of drug abuse. Some cannot function normally for the rest of their lives, even on medication. While others, if they refrain from using drugs, can live a normal life. Some children and teenagers overdose on drugs and eventually die.

The only safe way is not to touch, handle, or taste any form of harmful drugs. Some of the other drugs children and adolescents should avoid are tea, coffee, alcoholic wine, and foods that contain them. To refrain from these sinful practices, you must decide not to partake. In addition, you have to practice a devotional life, pray, and ask the Lord to resist temptations. It can sometimes be overwhelming, but avoid places and people that will tempt or influence you to engage you in the wrong behavior. Remember, God is always there to help you.

Sanballot, Tobiah, Arabians, Ammonites, and the Ashdodites heard that the walls of Jerusalem had been made up, and breaches began to be stopped. As a result, they became wrathful. All of them conspired together to fight against Jerusalem. Judah prayed to God and said they could not build the wall. The enemies of the Israelites wanted to come in, to slay them and cease the work. They would not let that happen, so the people were set in the high and low places after their families with swords, spears, and bows. Nehemiah told the people not to be afraid. They should remember the Lord, which is great and terrible. Fight for your brethren, sons and houses when the enemies heard that the people knew and God had bought their plans to naught. Everyone returned to the wall to continue building. Half of the persons worked, and another half stood guard with spears, shields, and bows. The builders and everyone had their swords girded by their sides. Nehemiah told the people, "When they hear the trumpet, God will fight for them." Nehemiah 4.

Use all your talents and abilities that God has given you to the honor and glory of God. Enjoy good habits and balance all healthful habits. Do not conceal your talent but use them to bless others. Make sure you balance all your health habits, not too much of any or not too little, just in the right proportion. . We should exercise self-control to choose the right foods and behavior. "But the fruit of the Spirit is love, joy, peace, longsuffering, gentleness, goodness, faith. Meekness, temperance: against such there is no law." Galatians 5: 22-23.

Dare to be a Daniel

Standing by a purpose true,

Heeding God's command,

Honor them, the faithful few!

All hail to Daniel's band!

Chorus

Dare to be a Daniel,

Dare to stand alone!

Dare to have a purpose firm!

Dare to make it known.

Many mighty men are lost,

Daring not to stand,

Who for God had been a host.

By joining Daniel's band.

Many giants, great and tall,

Stalking through the land,

Headlong to the earth would fall,

If met by Daniel's band.

Hold the Temperance banner high!

On to victory grand!

Satan and his hosts defy,

And shout for Daniel's band.

Air

In 2016, Alcides, a thirteen-year-old Peruvian boy, boarded a packed bus for a two-hour ride to the town to celebrate Peru's national holiday. Alcides was traveling on the bus that his elder brother Wilbur was driving. His brother was forty-five-year-old at the time. Three children stood in the hallway because all twenty-one seats were occupied. Wilbur halted the bus on the twisting, hilly road after driving for approximately thirty minutes. He was sleepy, so he threw water on his face from a nearby stream. Alcides felt sleepy as the bus proceeded, so he lay against the window and shut his eyes. As the bus moved around the curves, he noticed that the bus began to drive faster. Finally, the bus collided with a tree and tumbled down speeds around a bend. As the bus fell, Alcides doesn't recall hearing the passengers scream. Instead, he recalls the bus turning over and slamming his head on the window and the seats. "Please, God, help me. Don't let me die here," he prayed.

Quickly the bus split in half, and Alcides was thrown out. Suitcases, gas canisters, and beer boxes were raining out of the sky at him as he lay on his back. He prevented himself from getting hit by rolling backward and forward. He then heard the other passengers' screams. Fear overcame him, but he soon recognized that others required assistance. He approached a person who had a fractured leg. "You'll be OK," he stated. Immediately he recalled that his brother had been the bus driver. He went on a search for Wilbur and eventually located him. "What happened?" Wilbur said faintly. Alcides removed his shirt and wiped the blood from his brother's head. Then he discovered that he was the only one who hadn't been hurt.

The bus accident occurred close to a tiny village, and the residents responded by sending a car to assist the people. Then, somebody made a call to the mother of Wilbur and Alcides. She leaped on a horse and galloped to the accident site, arriving approximately in thirty minutes. She sobbed with relief when she saw Alcides. "You are alive because of God!" She cried, "Thank You, God!"

Police officers came and brought Alcides to the hospital for examination. At the same time, somebody else brought Wilbur to the hospital. Alcides was sent home after spending the night there. He was fine, according to the doctor. His sibling was moved to a bigger hospital in Cusco, where he underwent a number of surgeries. Many individuals who had never worshipped on the Sabbath gathered to hear Alcides' testimony when he went to his village's home church the next Sabbath. They also wanted to make sure he wasn't seriously injured. They were astonished. "It's a miracle. You are the only one who is uninjured," said someone. "You are the son of God because you were spared from death," said another person.

After hearing Alcides' miraculous testimony, six individuals were baptized. Because of Alcides, another seven persons study the Bible in preparation for baptism. A community member was so surprised that he donated property for the first Seventh Day Adventist church in the community to be built. He was baptized as well. His mother was so thankful to God for preserving her sons' lives that she raised funds to build the church. The church has twenty-five members who have been baptized. Wilbur has recovered completely, and Alcides is fifteen years old presently. He is currently praying for his brother to accept Jesus Christ in his life. Alcides aspires to be a mining engineer in the future. He remarks, however, that he will continually share his testimony with others about how God spared his life. "I think God spared me to be a testimony to other people," he said. "I never will stop sharing my love for Jesus and inviting people to Him."

Air played a vital role in the earth's creation and still influences our lives today. "And God said, let us make man in our image, after our likeness, and let them have dominion over the fish of the sea, and over the fowl of the air, and over the cattle, and over the earth, and over every creeping thing that creepeth upon the earth." Genesis 1:26. "And the Lord God formed man of the dust of the ground, and breathe into his nostrils the breath of life; and man became a living soul." Genesis 2:7. Human beings use air to engage in various activities. An interesting activity children and teens engage in is kite flying.

My brother and I used to create kites to fly in the air. We had sheets of paper formed into a square, triangle, or parallelogram shape with a stick. Then we would tie a long string to one of the sticks. We occasionally utilize tread, ropes, plastic, or anything else that can be used to construct a string. Each of us aspired to fly our kites higher than the other. It was sometimes challenging to manage, mainly when it was windy. The sun was sometimes scorching, but we didn't mind because we were more interested in how we flew our kites in the skies. I reasoned that God must have seen our kites and admired how we were soaring them.

We should always strive to have a higher experience with God in our lives, just as the bird is always flying higher. So always try your best in whatever you're pursuing in life. When we have a close relationship with God, we aim to go to heaven when Jesus will be coming to take us there."For the Lord himself shall descend from heaven with a shout, with the voice of the archangel, and with the trump of God: and the dead in Christ shall rise first: Then we which are alive and remain shall be caught up together with them in the clouds, to meet the Lord in the air: and so shall we ever be with the Lord. Wherefore comfort one another with these words." 1 Thessalonians 4: 16-18.

As children, you should get as much fresh air as possible. Go outside your house for fresh air when the weather is favorable, and you're well enough to be outside. Do not sit around playing games on tablets, phones, or computers and watching shows inside. Instead, walk outside the house, especially in the morning, and engage in deep breathing, walking, or playing outdoors. This will keep you healthier in mind and body. You will also learn about your environment. When you are ill and unable to be outside, open your windows to gain fresh air.

Human beings require air to survive. We could live for weeks without food or days without water, but we would die in minutes if we were starved of oxygen. Therefore, the body must have oxygen. All the cells require a consistent, fresh oxygen supply to function efficiently. Each day you inhale approximately 17,000 breaths. The heart transports blood to the lungs, where carbon dioxide is expelled, and fresh oxygen is taken in to be delivered to all of the body's cells.

The benefits of fresh air are numerous. It promotes learning and thinking capacity and improves the brain's ability to function normally. It stimulates the brain's serotonin hormone (good feeling hormone) levels, causing a joyful feeling and good health. It helps you to sleep better and destroy germs in the atmosphere. On the other hand, when the air is polluted, it deprives the body of fresh air.

Air pollutants have different effects on people. The signs and symptoms are allergies, sadness, dizziness, tiredness, coughing, burning eyes and sore throat, anxiety, headache, restlessness, depression, and nausea. Pollution has also been linked to an increase in asthma, other respiratory disorders, cancer, and other ailments caused by many pollutants.

Impure air can be breathed and re-breathed when in enclosed spaces. The quantity of oxygen in the atmosphere declines while carbon dioxide and other wastes rise. The oxygen supply in this polluted air is insufficient to preserve the cells' functioning. Pure air helps to prevent illnesses and death. In addition, pure air helps the body eliminate waste. Waste is effectively disposed of when the volume of air is adequate.

While fresh air is essential for everyone, it is even more vital for the bedridden sick. If the patient does not get sufficient fresh air, it will take longer to heal or may never recover. For example, if a wound does not have adequate air, it will not heal. In addition, engaging in a deep breathing exercise can assist the individual in confidence, fear and relaxes the nervous system.

God intended for us to breathe pure air from the moment we were born until we died, without taking a minute off.

Ezekiel Saw the Wheels

Better mind, my sister, how you walk on the cross,

Way up in the middle of the air.

Your foot might slip and your soul be lost,

Way up in the middle of the air.

Ezekiel saw the wheels,

Way up in the middle of the air.

Ezekiel saw the wheels,

Way up in the middle of the air.

And the big wheel run by faith,

And the little wheel runs by the Grace of God.

In the wheel, in the wheel,

Way up in the middle of the air.

Let me tell you, brother, what a sinner will do,

Way up in the middle of the air.

He'll talk about me, and he'll talk about you,

Way up in the middle of the air.

Trust in God

Namoonga dropped out of school when she was thirteen years old. She couldn't move from the sofa to the door of her home in Lusaka, Zambia's capital. She sat on the sofa by the open window, fighting to breathe because the room was always stifling. Namoonga lacked the energy to study. She was unable to read or write. She grew slender as she sat by the window. Namoonga lacked the energy to study, so her parents and friends prayed for her. They talked about their concerns honestly. "This girl is going to die," someone said. "The doctors can't operate on her," said another person. "She is too thin."

After a series of testing by the physicians, they stated that Namoonga had a leaking heart valve, so it had to be replaced. In addition, she needed to have an open-heart surgery done. "I was told I had to undergo an operation, and that was the only way to get better," she stated. Her surgery would be done at the University Teaching Hospital, located in Lusaka. However, Namoonga had to wait for the arrival of competent surgeons from Russia first. Russian doctors visited the hospital twice a year to do open-heart surgery.

As she waited, Namoonga's health deteriorated. She was admitted to the hospital regularly. She was admitted two times in the same week on multiple occasions after her legs were swollen. The Russian medical doctors finally came. "God, I am ready to go to the operation," Namoonga prayed to God as she was brought into the operating room where doctors would do her surgery. "Whatever happens, let it happen. Let it be according to your will."

The complex operation took eight hours to complete. The surgeons carefully removed the leaky heart valve and replaced it with a metal valve. Namoonga requested a glass of water as soon as she awoke. She was exhausted and feeble. When she looked around the hospital room, she noticed equipment everywhere. Then she saw her family, who were all ready to hug her. Namoonga was transported from the intensive care unit to a typical hospital room three days later. The doctors remarked that the surgery was a success, but the physicians warned Namoonga that she would need to take heart medication daily for the rest of her life.

Namoonga went back to school some months after the surgery. The operation took place ten years ago. Namoonga is now 24 years old and a fourth-year student attending Rusangu University. She plans to start an organization to assist children with heart problems after graduation.

Surgery and medicine are vital, but only God deserves the credit for preserving her life, according to Namoonga. She stated, "God gave me life and is keeping me." Namoonga's words endorse Revelation 4: 11, which says, "You are worthy, our Lord and God, to receive glory, honor and power, for you created all things, and by your will, they were created and have their being" (NIV). "God has been there since the beginning," Namoonga said. "It was not the medicine that helped me get better. It was God keeping me. It is not because of the metal valve that I am still alive. It is God keeping me alive all the time."

I learned as a child how significant it is to reverence God and how powerful he is if we sincerely trust and obey him. Pastor Harold Campbell shared the story of how criminals stole some lovely chairs that were from the church he pastored. One Sabbath evening, church members prayed for the chairs to be returned. The members eventually witnessed each of the stolen chairs being lowered one by one with a rope in the churchyard. They didn't see any faces, but they got all the chairs back. They never took anything else from that church again during that time. When we pray, we should trust God to answer our prayers. "Trust in the Lord with all thine heart; and lean not unto thine own understanding. In all thy ways acknowledge him, and he shall direct thy paths." Proverbs 3: 5-6.

Pray and read God's word daily to develop a closer relationship with Jesus. The Bible shows the character of God and the loving Savior who died for mankind. Children and teenagers who read the Bible and pray know that God is always there to care for and support them during challenging times. If you cannot do academic work, experience abuse, suffering from an incurable disease, pray and trust in God because he loves and cares for you. Never stop praying and trusting God; He will always answer your prayers. Your prayers are not necessarily answered the way you want them to be, but he will always answer them.

Jehovah sent Jesus, his only son, into this world as a babe born of a virgin called Mary and his father, Joseph. He was baptized by John the Baptist. In his ministry on earth, Jesus did many miracles; he fed the hungry, loved everyone, cared for all, was kind, and was crucified after he had done so many beautiful acts for men. Boys and girls, Jesus died for everyone so we can have eternal life. He gives each one a protecting angel to guide us so that his presence will always be with us.

"But God commendeth his love toward us, in that, while we were yet sinners, Christ died for us." Romans 5:8. He promised that he would return for his faithful children. He is still in heaven, watching over his children and caring for them. He still guides and has his protection over his little children. The heavenly father understands the end from the beginning and knows what is best for us. Therefore, when the trying times come, be continuous in praying; never stop because God will be there for you through his words and give you the strength to cope.

The only action that God has toward us is love. God's love, with its infinite wisdom, assures us that whatever he does for his children is well done. Through trials and temptations, we know Christ. These difficulties are there to strengthen us to become better individuals. We should never be sad and hurt but be grateful to be a part of the sufferings of Christ. When we cannot bear them, we have a friend in Jesus that will assist us. We need not be worried because his plans are perfect. If it means that you will die when your life is in his hands, you will die in Christ, and you know that when Christ returns, you will be ready to go to heaven with him. Sometimes standing for Jesus can even cause death, but rest assured, when your life is in God's hands, you have no need to be fear of death. "For whosoever will save his life shall lose it: and whosoever will lose his life for my sake shall find it." Matthew 16:25. Make sure your life is in harmony with his. "But even the very hairs of your head are all numbered. Fear not therefore: ye are of more value than many sparrows." Luke 12:7.

The enemy Satan allowed Adam and Eve to sin by tempting them. After that, sin prevailed; in the world, it still exists. Because of the enemy, we experience these painful times like sickness and death, but God allows it to happen. Despite these struggles, God can carry us through all of these circumstances.

Prayer is openly speaking to God as you would relate to your friend. Share with him, your problems, worries, desires, happiness, and difficulties. Persist in knowing about Him and conversing with Him. You will discover His great eternal love, strength and knowledge, compassion, magnificence, and the happiness of performing out His will. You will believe in Him and understand that He cherishes you and will never hurt you.

Jabez's name meant I bore in pain. Probably his mother bore him in pain. Because of his name, he didn't want to cause any pain. "And Jabez was more honorable than his brethren: and his mother called his name Jabez, saying, Because I bore him with sorrow." 1 Chronicles 4:9. Jabez prayed to his heavenly Father to bless him abundantly, enlarge his coast, and protect him from evil. God granted Jabez what he requested. He would be a blessing and not a curse. 1 Chronicles 4:10. "Delight thyself also in the Lord: and he shall give thee the desires of thine heart. Commit thy way unto the Lord; trust also in him, and he shall bring it to pass." Psalm 37: 4-5.

Be thankful to God for everything, in good times and bad times. Remember to help others because you help yourself in doing it will prove a blessing. The Lord always has plans for his beautiful children. "For I know the thoughts that I think toward you, saith the Lord, thoughts of peace, and not of evil, to give you an expected end. Then shall ye call upon me, and ye shall go and pray unto me, and I will hearken unto you." Jeremiah 29: 11-12.

Fill my Cup Let it Overflow with Love

Fill my cup, let it overflow (fill it up),

Fill my cup, let it overflow,

Fill my cup, let it overflow,

Let it overflow with love.

Jesus loves me, this I know (this I know),

For the Bible tells me so,

Little ones to him belong,

They are weak, but he is strong.

Fill my cup, let it overflow (fill it up),

Fill my cup, let it overflow,

Fill my cup, let it overflow,

Let it overflow with love.

Amazing grace; how sweet the sound (sweet the sound),

That saved a wretch like me one day,

I once was lost, but now I'm found,

I was blind, but now I see.

Fill my cup, let it overflow (fill it up).

Fill my cup, let it overflow,

Fill my cup, let it overflow,

Let it overflow with love.

Peace

When the family of Ann discovered that she had given her life to Jesus, a conflict arose. Ann's family took her Bible and other books away from her. She requested that they return her books, but they informed her they did not have them. So Ann went to a Christian church and requested a new Bible, but her family also snatched this one. Afterwards, she concealed the Bible and secretly read it. On the other hand, Ann's relatives knew she continued reading the Bible. Finally, her father slapped her and told her to stop reading the scriptures. Ann's uncle went so far as to make a threat to kill her. Ann was terrified and unsure of what to do.

"Blessed are you when they revile and persecute you, and say all kinds of evil against you falsely for my sake," Jesus says, "Rejoice and be exceedingly glad, for great is your reward in heaven, for so they persecuted the prophets who were before you." Matthew 5:11-12 (NKJV). Ann discovered that Christians should be baptized in the Bible when she became older. She desired to be baptized but had no idea which church she should attend. Ann asked herself, which church is the true one? Ann studied the Bible constantly for two months because she was desperate to figure out what God intended for her to do. "I do not know where to be baptized," she cried out to God one day as she fell on her knees with pain in her heart. "Where can I find your true Christians?" Ann heard a small voice inside her say, "A true Christian is someone who keeps the Ten Commandments." She was aware that God was guiding her.

Ann wanted to locate a congregation that followed the Ten Commandments of God, which made sense to her. Ann knew the commandments, such as "Do not kill." "Do not steal." "Honor your father and mother." Many Christian churches follow these commandments. The Fourth Commandment, on the other hand, worried her. What is the meaning of the fourth commandment? "Remember the Sabbath to keep it holy." The Fourth commandment meant to Ann, coming to church on Saturday to celebrate Jesus. However, she was unaware of any Christian churches that keep their services on Saturdays. All the churches that she was aware of worship on Sundays.

She found an article about the Seventh-day Adventist Church while one day browsing the Internet. According to what she read, Adventists follow all Ten Commandments, including the fourth. So, Ann looked up the address of an Adventist church in her hometown on the Internet. She discovered a church and went to speak with the church's pastor. Ann told him about her conversion to Jesus Christ, and they both studied the Bible together, and she eventually was baptized into God's true church at long last! She can't give you her actual name since being a Christian in my country is unsafe. Many individuals would threaten to kill her if they discovered she had changed from her family's religion to Christianity. Although being a Christian is risky, Ann will not change her stance even if she is beaten, intimidated, or murdered. She loves Jesus Christ and will always be obedient to Him. She has peace because of Jesus.

Nabal was a wealthy man; he was married to Abigail, who was a good woman. Nabal was an evil man with three thousand sheep and a thousand goats. David had helped Nabal before and heard he was shearing sheep. David sent ten men to Nabal for food. Nabal answered and asked who David was. He asked if he should take the bread, water, and flesh he had killed for his shears and give food to them. He said he never knew where they came from. David's servants went and told him what Nabal had said. David decided to make war with Nabal. One of David's servants told Abigail what her husband did to David's servants.

Abigail hurriedly took two hundred loaves, two bottles of wine, five sheep, five measures of parched corn, hundred clusters of raisins, and two hundred cakes of figs. She and her servants left to go to David, but she never told her husband. After seeing how she greeted and treated him. He decided he wouldn't go to war with Nabal because she had made peace. Abigail told her husband what David had planned, and his heart failed to function, and he lay dying. Ten days after the incident, the Lord killed him, and then Abigail became David's wife. 1 Samuels 25.

A peacemaker will show Christ's love to others through the calm influence of a pure life. For example, through their words and actions, children will encourage other persons to stop doing sinful activities and give their lives to Jesus Christ, who is the peacemaker. If you agree to give up sinful behaviors and surrender your life to Jesus Christ, you will receive Jesus' love and will be able to participate in the everlasting peace of your savior.

Only in Jesus, you can find peace. When the peace of God is taken into the heart, you will have no hatred, no fights with anyone, and your mind will be full of love for others. You always will remain calm and patient. You will never be a miserable child or teen if you are at peace with God and everyone. No jealousy will exist; evil thinking and hate will not be in the heart. The peace of God in your life will spread its blessings to those around you. For children and adolescents who are tired and troubled by wars in their society, the peace of God will fall like raindrops on them when they give their hearts to Jesus. The peace of God will bring comfort to these hurting ones. The children of God will share the message of peace throughout the world.

"Blessed are the peacemakers: for they shall be called the children of God." Matthew 5:9. The peace of God in children's lives shows that they have a relationship with their heavenly father; this can be seen in adults and children. The sweet aroma of Christ circles them. The perfume of their lives and the beauty of their behaviors show the world that they are God's beautiful children.

We should, if possible, live at peace with all men. Romans 12:18. When anyone seeks to make conflict with you and refuses to resolve it, it is always best to walk away and pray to God to assist you. If it is not a situation you can walk away, try to find someone to talk to about the matter. If you cannot speak to anyone, you should pray to God. He can resolve all our conflicts. It might not be the time in which we want it to happen. He can manage every situation in his time. Never try to make war and strife. Try to live a peaceful life. Jesus is a gentleman, and he never tried to make any war. He is our example; we should follow him. If you are in a situation that you cannot cope with, take it to the Lord in prayer, and he will help you solve your conflict. "Peace I leave with you, my peace I give unto you: not as the world giveth, give I unto you. Let not your heart be troubled, neither let it be afraid." John 14: 27.

Peacespeaker

It was such a lovely day,

And the sun was shining bright.

A gentle breeze was blowing my way,

Not a storm cloud in sight.

Then suddenly, without a warning,

A storm surrounded my life.

But even in the storm,

I can feel the calm,

And here's the reason why.

I know the Peacespeaker;

I know Him by name.

I know the Peacespeaker;

He controls the winds and waves.

When He says, "Peace, be still,"

They have to obey.

I'm glad I know the Peacespeaker.

Yes, I know Him by name;

There's never been another man,

With the power of this friend,

By simply saying, "Peace, be still."

He can calm the strongest wind,

So now, I'll never worry.

When storm clouds come my way,

I know that He is near,

To drive away my fear,

And I can smile and say,

I know the Peacespeaker,

I know Him by name.

I know the Peacespeaker,

He controls the winds and waves.

When He says, "Peace, be still,"

They have to obey.

I'm glad I know the Peacespeaker.

Yes, I know Him by name,

Peace, peace wonderful peace,

Coming down from the Father above.

When he says, "Peace, be still,"

They have to obey.

I'm glad I know the Peacespeaker.

Yes, I know Him by name.

I'm glad I know the Peacespeaker.

Yes, I know Him by name.

Forgiveness

"Forgiveness is a willful act, and the will may function regardless of the heart's temperature." She was speaking from her personal experience. This little church in Northern Germany was the last place Corrie Ten Boom expected to be, but it was also the first place she felt called. As she talked to the people about the love of God and forgiveness, the numerous wounds inflicted by the Nazi dictatorship were still burning in her heart. She had only recently been imprisoned in the Ravensbruck concentration camp some months before, one of World War II's most dangerous and horrific camps, where her precious sister, Betsy, had perished along with countless other females. Only twenty percent of the females who came through the camp gates ever lived to see another day of freedom in this camp.

Corrie reflected on eight months before, as the German congregation in front of Corrie vanished behind the memories of the terrible cold night, Betsy was snatched from her. Betsy's fragile, chilly fingers on Corrie's hand still chilled her. Her brilliant blue eyes reflected her last words to Corrie, inspired by the love of God. "Remember, dear sister," she whispered gently, "No pit is so deep that God's love is not deeper still."

Corrie spent a restless night beside her deceased sister, Betsy, replaying the brutal beating she had received at the hands of a German guard. Corrie could still see anger in the steely blue eyes of a cruel man utterly captivated by a spirit that was nothing like her dear sister. Much like a robber who had taken millions, the guard had returned for the pennies that were left. Corrie's heart was ripped apart by the quiet cries of rage and fervent prayers for forgiveness, as her heart fought a conflict as if one was tearing the world apart outside. Even while she suffered at the hands of her foe, Betsy declared the forgiveness of God for him. Corrie prayed to God for the same kind of spirit.

The terrible memories disappeared, and a flood of German faces appeared in their place. "We all are adversaries of Christ, and yet his forgiveness is offered freely." She persisted, "As we ought to offer forgiveness to one another, no matter how great or small the offense." After the service, Corrie stood outside the church doors, talking with the people leaving the church building. Her heart swelled with gratitude and then came to a halt as she eagerly shook hands and exchanged pleasantries with these people who had only recently been enemies.

Her convictions about forgiveness shook as firmly as her hands as she was stopped in her tracks by a face in the crowd. A few moments later, the piercing blue eyes that had blazed with scorn for her sister were looking into her face. The hatred, though, had faded. In its place, there was a deep sense of grief and fear. "Forgive me, Miss Ten Boom," he said quietly, reaching out a trembling hand to her. "Please," Corrie said, raising her hand to grab the hand of the man who had murdered her sister after observing the man for some time with a difficult glance, "Forgiveness no matter the temperature of the heart," she told herself. Tears of joy and relief filled up both of their eyes. Corrie had learnt the important lesson of God's love and forgiveness.

A father had two sons. The younger son decided that he wanted his father to give him his portion of goods. The father gave him his own, and he went to a faraway country. He lived a riotous life and squandered what his father gave him. He lost all his possession and became in need of everyday amenities. There was a famine in the country in which he went to live. The only form of employment he could find was taking care of pigs. He also ate the pigs' food. When he thought about how his father had servants and a wealthy lifestyle, he decided to return home.

While returning home, his father saw him far away. He had compassion on him and ran, fell on his neck, and kissed him. The son told him he had sinned against him and was not worthy of being called his son. He should treat him as one of his hired servants. The father told his servant to bring the best robe and put it on him; a ring was set on one of his finger, and a pair of shoes on his feet. A fat calf should be killed, and they should have a feast and be happy. He said his other son was dead; his lost son was found and alive. Luke 15: 11-

32. "But if ye forgive not men their trespasses, neither will your Father forgive your trespasses." Matthew 6:15.

If you forgive others, you will receive forgiveness from God, but you will not receive forgiveness from Jesus Christ if you do not forgive others. The source of all forgiveness is God's love, but our behavior towards others will show if we have a love of God in our hearts. You have no excuse not to forgive others. If you do not have mercy for others, it shows that you do not have a love of God in your heart. When you have a love of God in your heart, you will forgive others and become closer to Jesus. You will have the kindness of God, and it will overflow to people. Allow Christ to live in your hearts so you can share his love and bring hope to the hopeless. As we grow with Jesus, we will get more compassion and show people these Christ-like behaviors.

When we are hurt, we should never be revengeful towards those who harm us or those who hurt us. Instead, we should learn to forgive anyone that has hurt us. Jesus forgives us for our sins, showing us that we should do the same. When his disciples asked him how often we should forgive. He told them seventy times seven. It can be physically, emotionally, and spiritually painful when we are hurt. Sometimes, we want to fight back; we hoard the pain and are unwilling to let go. We should forgive our friends, family, or anyone who has done us wrong to be free. "Then came Peter to him, and said, Lord, how oft shall my brother sin against me, and I forgive him? Till seven times? Jesus saith unto him, I say not unto thee, until seven times: but, until seventy times seven." Matthew 18: 21-22.

The Lord's Prayer

Our Father, who art in heaven,

Hallowed be thy Name,

Thy kingdom come,

Thy will be done,

On earth as it is in heaven.

Give us this day our daily bread.

And forgive us our trespasses,

As we forgive those,

Who trespass against us.

And lead us not into temptation,

But deliver us from evil.

For thine is the kingdom,

And the power, and the glory,

for ever and ever. Amen.

Love

Andy did not have many things in his life, but he had two precious little children and the small cabin that they lived in. His wife abandoned the family many years ago, and he later discovered that she had remarried and died in an accident. Andy loved those little ones! And how well he looked after them! When the children weren't at the one-room schoolhouse down the road, they worked together on their small mountain farm. But then a tragic incident took place one day.

When the fire broke out, Andy was working in the fields. The girls were present in the house that morning. He fled as soon as he spotted the smoke. Suzy and Cindy, his dear little ones! He prayed as he sprinted across the field and then through a wooded area, knowing God would answer his prayer from previous experience.

The small cabin was engulfed in flames when he came. He rushed inside, hammering the door down with his strong shoulder, and discovered a blazing beam blocking another door. Throwing the door aside with only his hands, he entered the room and realized his girls were on the floor. They had been overpowered by the smoke while attempting to contain the fire. He grabbed them up with his powerful arms and ran out of the burning cabin. The building rafters collapsed behind him into the building as he stepped onto the outdoor porch. Despite the sparks, smoke, and flames that seemed everywhere, he managed to escape the fire into the yard.

They were unharmed. When the local magistrate heard about the situation, he decided that Andy's children should be separated from him and given to suitable people who could provide them with a better place. The whole town was in turmoil, and the courthouse was crowded on the day of the custody trial. The county attorney took the stand first and explained why he believed Andy's girls should be removed from him. People looked up to him because he was powerful and knowledgeable. On the other hand, Andy stood up. He could not afford to hire a lawyer to defend his case, so he defended himself. He testified about his love and care for his children over the years, his eyes filled with tears. He devoted his entire life to them despite the trials he faced.

As he closed his defense, he raised his hands and pleaded for his children to return to him. Both hands were marred by reddened, unsightly scars since they had been badly burned while rescuing his children. The courtroom became quiet at this time, and the judge attempted to talk but struggled to speak. Finally, he stated, "Andy was willing to give his life for his children, and he will carry the scars of his sacrifice in his hands for the remainder of his life. There is no one in this county better qualified to have them. This court rules that the children shall be given back to Andy."

The courtroom erupted in a burst of laughter for him. Andy showed love for his children more than anyone in the world, he had demonstrated himself willing to offer his life to save his precious girls and would reunite with them again. Andy's behavior represents the love of Christ. Christ gave his life to save us from sin.

There are different types of love, but I will highlight four different types of love.

Agape love is given freely; it is unconditional and selfless love. Jesus showed this kind of love for all humans. He was altruistic and sacrificed Himself so that others could be rid of their sins. Jesus bore the pain for humanity to be happy. Today, he continues to love and care for us. Eros is affiliated with romantic, passionate, and sexual love. This is the love that expresses sexual love and desire. Philia love is associated with brotherly love for each other. This is the love we express for each other. Philautia is the love you have for yourself. It is not being selfish, negative or unhealthy. Persons have to love themselves so they can love others and receive love from others.

The love we should have for each other is the philia love. We should love each other no matter the class, color, disabled, or background the person comes from. Your love should have no limitations; it should flow naturally for each other. We should always try to love those who are weakest around us. Love others by saying a kind word, a smile, a gesture or treating others well. Jesus showed the example of true love, the agape love. While he was on earth, he cared for everyone; they were so happy to be healed and fed by him. We should also care for others and pray for them when we cannot assist them. Feed the needy and offer assistance where you see it possible. It could be helping a sick family member or friend. We were made to love, so we should demonstrate it daily.

I accompanied my mother in visiting the sick and shut-ins close to our church. Each week my father would bake bread, and we would carry it for these elderly persons or persons who needed it at church. Sometimes, it was wearisome because these people had a lot to say, and at times, I couldn't understand why they had so much to say. But I later realized that I would face similar obstacles in my life. What they had to say was relevant and assisted in my decision-making. The Sabbath school teacher would take us to shut-ins, and we would have Sabbath school class with them, praying and singing. Those lessons taught me how to treat the elderly, the disabled, and the less fortunate. They have feelings and need love like everyone else. We should treat them with love and care. A blessing will await you, not necessarily from them but from God. "For all the law is fulfilled in one word, even in this; Thou shall love thy neighbor as thyself." Galatians 5:14.

Sherie had an interesting experience as a teenager. There was an elderly woman who was attending her church. The Holy Spirit impressed her to pay attention to the elderly woman. The elderly woman had no friends at church. She was always miserable. Whenever a child bothered her, she would lift her stick at the individual, and the child would walk away. Sherie befriended the elderly woman. One Sabbath afternoon, when the morning service ended, the elderly lady said, "Please, for two dollars". Sherie did not have any money to give the lady but when she went home, she told her mother about the situation. Mother said, "If she is asking for two dollars, she is hungry."

The next Sabbath, Sherie and her mother visited the elderly woman and gave her a meal. The elderly lady appreciated the meal and said she was hungry for many days. Each Sabbath, Sherie and her mother gave the elderly woman a meal and had worship with her. The mother would also visit her weekly to see how she was doing. This relationship with the elderly woman continued until she died. Sherie never forget this experience. Children and teenagers should learn to care for the elderly and listen when the Holy Spirit speaks to them.

Jacob journeyed through the land of Haran. His mother's brother Laban lived there with his two daughters, Rachel and Leah. When he came there, Laban servants were caring for the flocks; he also saw Rachel. Leah had a lazy eye. Laban greeted Jacob, and they were happy to see each other. Jacob decided to stay with his uncle. After staying there for a while, he fell in love with Rachel. He asked Laban if he could marry her. Laban told him, since there were relatives, he would agree for him to marry Rachel. However, he would have to stay seven years and work for her. He decided to stay for those years because he had fallen in love with her. After all, she was beautiful.

After seven years of working to have Rachel as his wife, Jacob went to Laban for Rachel. After a big feast, Leah was presented to him as his wife and a maid. Jacob was so disappointed with what his uncle did to him. Laban had tricked him into believing he would have Rachel for his wife. Jacob went and told Laban what he had done; he told Jacob, in that country, the first daughter would marry first, so he gave Leah to him. He told him he had to work another seven years for Rachel. He would have to work fourteen years for Rachel to marry her.

After the other seven years he had worked, Rachel was given him with a maid. Jacob loved her so much that he worked so long to have her for his wife. True love waits; we should love each other as Christ loved us. Jacob manifested true love for his wife; we should also manifest true love for each other. Genesis 29.

"For God so loved the world that he gave his only begotten Son, that whosoever believeth in him should not perish, but have everlasting life." John 3: 16. "But God commendeth his love towards us, in that, while we were yet sinners, Christ died for us." Romans 5: 8. Treat someone kind today, it could be that individual that will save your life later. Never mistreat anyone, have respect for everyone you come in contact with, and love everyone.

The best gift our heavenly father has ever given to his children is his wonderful love. If you do not have a close relationship with Jesus, you cannot have love. "We love Him, because He first loved us." 1 John 4:19. When you have a love of Jesus in your life, it rules your behavior. You will have a changed heart and not practice unruly behavior. God's love is a treasure that refreshes life and positively influences everyone you encounter. Love is the source of purity. If you are selfish, you do not have love for people. When your life is united with Christ, love pours out naturally to everyone.

When one's self is fused with Christ, love comes naturally. The willingness to help and bless others always flows from the heart.

When the love of heaven fills the mind, it is seen in the face, and Christ-like behavior is fully shown. When we are united with Christ, we are linked to others by the golden cords of love. Children and teenagers should be kind and helpful to those in need and suffering, similar to how Christ did well. The love of God cannot be measured and is never fully understood. But you are expected to show it to each other. No matter how persons are unkind to you, do not stop showing love to them. This love is pure and holy; you have to build this love each day with Christ, so you can naturally give it to people despite their unkindness.

Love is something if you give it away

Love is something if you give it away,

Give it away, give it away.

Love is something if you give it away,

You end up having more.

It's just like a magic penny,

Hold it tight, and you won't have any.

Lend it, spend it, and you'll have so many,

They'll roll all over the floor.

Money's dandy, and we like to use it.

But love is better if you don't refuse it.

It's a treasure, and you'll never lose it

Unless you lock up your door.

So let's go dancing till the break of the day,

And if there's a piper, we can pay.

For love is something, if you give it away,

You end up having more.

Faith

Soldiers destroyed many people's property during the First World War in Europe in 1914. A wealthy lady from Russia was among those who suffered the loss of possession. She was a Russian aristocrat. Her friends called her "The Princess" because of her lofty existence. When the military arrived, they demolished her home and stole all her money, which was roughly $50,000. Her son was murdered, and his wife died from a contagious disease. They left behind three girls; their ages were fourteen, eight, and six years old to care for. She and her grandchildren had to work from sunrise until night to earn sufficient funds to purchase a loaf of bread and milk. The work eventually ended after a while, and they appeared to be on the verge of starvation. Finally, a day came when the family had their last meal and did not know how they would survive.

"We have nothing for lunch tonight," stated the little girl. "What shall we do, Grandmother?" "The Great Father will take care of us, my darling," the grandmother responded. Then the family knelt and asked their heavenly Father to provide a meal for their supper. "Dear Lord, don't send us just a piece of bread; send us a whole loaf. For you know, Lord, we need a whole loaf," this was the petition of her youngest grandchild. In the afternoon, they conducted their usual tasks. When evening arrived, they did not have anything to eat, and the family had no funds to purchase food. The family set the empty table and sat around it. "Shall we thank the Great Father for the food before we see it?" The grandchildren inquired. "Yes," Grandmother responded.

The grandchildren were confident that God would provide food for them. They put their hands together and bowed their heads in gratitude. Then they heard a knocking on the door. When they unlocked the door, they saw a family friend who knew them when they were wealthy. He was a rich man also, but the war stole his possessions. So he walked over eighteen miles through heavy snow to visit the family. He had spent the entire afternoon walking. "I hardly know why I have come," he stated while he walked into the house. "But I felt that I ought to visit my old friend." Then, turning to the girls, he said to them, "Children, you don't know what I have brought you."

"Yes, we do!" Answered one of the girls, smiling. "What have I brought?" The man inquired.

"You have brought us a loaf of bread, not a piece of bread, but a whole loaf," the girl responded. "Well, well!" Answered the family friend, "How did you know that?" "Because we prayed to God to send us a loaf of bread," the small child stated, "And we asked Him to send us a full, large loaf, for we needed it." "Well," said the visitor, "That is just what I have brought. So now I know why I came." Then, beneath his large jacket, he took out one long loaf that European bakers produce. Indeed, God had sent him in response to a small child's request. "Now faith is the substance of things hoped for, the evidence of things not seen." Hebrews 11:1.

Jesus compared the kingdom of God to a man traveling to a far land and giving his servants goods. He gave one of his servants five talents, the other two talents, and another one. He gave them according to their abilities. The servant who got five added five more talents. The one who got two talents added two more. The one who got one talent hid his talent. After a long time, the master came; when he asked how many talents the one who had got five and the one who got two, they doubled their talents. The master said, well done, good and faithful servant, thou hast been faithful over few things you can enter into the joy of thy Lord. Matthew 25:14-23.

God gives everyone different talents. We should be satisfied with the gifts God gives us. We should never envy anyone for their talents. If we have faith and use what God has for us, he will bless us more. Faith believes it will happen even though we might never see the outcome. We worship God by faith. We never see him, but we believe he exists and works the best for our lives. We should exhibit such faith every day with our friends and family and believe that God will help us do our best to have in Christ as we live our lives. "Therefore I say unto you, what things soever ye desire, when ye pray, believe that ye receive them, and ye shall have them." Mark 11: 24.

You must think about faith, speak faith, and act in faith to grow in faith. As you exercise living faith, you will blossom into powerful boys and girls in Jesus Christ. You should spread hope, faith, and the light of Christ to others. You are not to grumble about His service as if He is a harsh teacher heaping duties on you that you cannot handle. It is not what Christ means. He wishes you to be filled with happiness, with His blessings, and to understand God's love's depth, thickness, greatness, and deepness, which is beyond human understanding. When you call on Jesus in faith, especially when facing problems, He will respond. If a dog attacks you, a thief, or anyone else, call on the name of Jesus in faith, pray in faith and sing in faith, reading the Bible in faith and God will answer you.

Find us Faithful

We're pilgrims on the journey,

Of the narrow road,

And those who've gone before us line the way,

Cheering on the faithful, encouraging the weary,

Their lives, a stirring testament to God's sustaining grace,

Surrounded by so great a cloud of witnesses.

Let us run the race not only for the prize,

But as those who've gone before us;

Let us leave to those behind us,

The heritage of faithfulness passed on through godly lives.

CHORUS:

Oh, may all who come behind us find us faithful,

May the fire of our devotion light their way,

May the footprints that we leave,

Lead them to believe,

And the lives we live inspire them to obey.

Oh, may all who come behind us find us faithful,

After all our hopes and dreams have come and gone,

And our children sift through all we've left behind,

May the clues that they discover and the memories they uncover,

Become the light that leads them to the road we each must find.

Protection

Amanda was a young Waldensian girl who lived in the Piedmont valleys of Northern Italy in the Middle Ages. Like what occurred centuries before, whoever owned or read a Bible near the end of the Middle Ages would receive the death penalty if they were caught.

Throughout centuries of persecution, the Waldenses kept Bibles hidden in secret for hundreds of years. The Waldenses read and memorized the scriptures and discreetly gave them out throughout Europe to people who could read. Several Waldenses were captured and martyred for their faith. Crusades (papal armies) were sent out on many occasions to kill all the Waldenses, but God always protected a few Waldenses.

Their faithful witnessing of God's word and the Bibles they gave to people eventually resulted in the reformation and religious liberty across Europe. Amanda's mother lovingly taught her the precious gems of the Bible that she had learned from her mother. She had memorized a vast number of Scriptures since she was a child. She was also taught the value of secrecy and the risk of possessing such an excellent book. The army's finding meant death, but reading and obeying it meant eternal life.

It happened one day quite unexpectedly. Her father left home while her mother was making the bread dough, preparing to place it in pans, and then baking them in the oven. Mother had her Bible open on the table, as she always did when she did not see anybody. At this time, she would frequently memorize the scriptures. Amanda heard hoof pounding coming around the trail to their valley house at the foot of the mountains that very moment. Before she even heard the sound, the soldiers were on the spot. She peered out just in time to see two soldiers leaping from their horses in front of the door of her home. "Mother!" She said frighteningly, "Mother, they are soldiers!"

She didn't have to say anything else. The soldiers never knocked on the door; instead, they pushed the door open and marched in, searching for the Bible. If they were caught, it meant the death penalty, and Amanda knew they had been found! There was no time to conceal the Bible because it was right there on the table. "Where is the Book!" The soldiers requested. "You have been reported as having a Bible. Turn it over to us now." Amanda was frightened at this moment. Indeed, the opened Bible could be seen clearly on the table. She turned to face her mother, but the Bible was nowhere to be found! What happened to it? All she saw was her mother calmly placing the last pan of bread in the oven as if it was routine, and she couldn't be disturbed until the bread was baked safely.

Mother simply turned around and remarked, "I do not know who could have reported such a thing. You will not find a Bible in this house. You can search if you like." "Why, Mother!" She exclaimed. Amanda was thinking about this, as she had been taught never to lie by her mom. Of course, her mother had not lied if the soldiers could not locate the Bible, but how could she be so sure? Amanda was perplexed as to how her mother could be so peaceful. How did Mother conceal it so fast? And where did she put it? Mother did not move away from where she was kneading the bread to put in the oven to be baked. She couldn't think about it because it was too big a mystery. While a soldier watched Amanda and her mother, the other began ransacking the home.

Amanda stood there in awe as he went from corner to corner, not missing a single place. He examined every board on the floor and each piece of wood on the walls to see if there was a secret hidden area. The soldier had previously done this before in other Waldensean homes. Finally, he arrived at Mother's kitchen, where she was baking bread. He could find the Bible now, for sure! He looked inside the firebox to see any traces of a burned book. Where could Mother have concealed it, and how had she kept so peaceful and relaxed? The soldier opened the cupboards and took out everything from them. When the soldier opened the oven door, he only saw loaves of bread baking. Amanda's mother reminded them, "I told you that you would not find a Bible in this house," Amanda had started to believe her mother. They eventually left, disappointed, believing they had got a false report to come to their house.

Amanda kept her breath until the horses were no longer able to hear. Amanda then asked, still fearfully speaking low, "Mother, where did you put the Bible?" "Let me take the bread out of the oven first. I was afraid; it might get too done before they left. There now, doesn't that look fine?" Amanda's Mother responded by lifting the first loaf of bread. "Isn't it wonderful how the Lord always provides for our needs? Dear, we must thank the Lord for protecting us, for surely, if He had not sent His angel we would have been caught." "But, Mother, where is the Bible? Did an angel really take it?"

"Not exactly, my dear," Mother responded. "But an angel did tell me what to do. Come, let us kneel and thank God for His protection."

"Now, dear," said Mother, rising from her knees, "We will have some fresh bread for supper when Father comes. He should be here shortly." Then, as though recalling the question of Amanda, she remarked, "You will find out about the Bible then." Amanda was now monitoring the path for Father.

When she saw him, she dashed over to tell him about the day's dramatic events. "Wherever Mother put the Bible, I do not know," Amanda started gasping. The home was still in shambles, but the table was arranged, and a loaf of bread sat in the center.

Mother did not have enough time to even the loaf properly before the soldiers arrived, so it wasn't the finest loaf of bread. Mother cut the bread after the blessing. Usually, Father would cut it, but Mother insisted she would do it this time. She cut through the crust with such care, almost solemnly, as if this loaf of bread were the most valuable thing on Earth.

"Mother! There is the Bible!" Amanda shouted excitedly. Mother carefully peeled the bread away from the priceless treasure. It appeared to be in perfect condition, as though miraculously saved.

"So that is what happened to the Bible!" said Amanda in awe. "You wrapped it in the bread dough and stuck it in the oven. Surely, if you had not been studying the Bible while making your bread, you could not have hidden it, and the soldiers would have found it."

"That is right," Mother replied. "When the soldiers came, I did not have time to even think. It was as if an angel spoke to me, and my hands immediately complied. I wrapped the Bible in the bread dough, put it in the last loaf pan, and put it into the oven. I would never have been able to think of it so quickly. Surely the Lord has protected us. "Put on the whole armour of God, that ye may be able to stand against the wiles of the devil." Ephesians 6: 11.

My siblings and I went to the market. While in the market, we heard gunshots firing. I started praying. It sounded so close to us that we took cover. However, when we completed buying, we went to take transportation home. While awaiting a bus, when we looked up the road, it was in total blackness because of the number of gunshots firing. The bag I had in my hand was light, but it felt heavier and heavier as if it could fall from my hand. My hands started shaking vigorously. Finally, the last bus came out, and we had to walk to another location for transportation. We saw a church brother we knew and asked him if he could carry us closer home, but he said he could not because he had to go shopping in the market. We asked him if we could wait, and he said no, as he was not going in our direction. While going, we started hearing gunshots we had to divert to another street. While walking, I continued praying. When we reached the other bus stop, only one bus was left. We were happy to get transportation home. God will always answer our prayers not how we want to but in the best way.

The Israelites had been enslaved in Egypt for over four-hundred years. God instructed Moses and Aaron to rescue his people. Moses went to Pharaoh to deliver God's people, but he refused. Plagues were cast on the Egyptians, but none ever affected the Israelites. All the firstborns were killed in the last plague, even the cattle. But the Israelites had blood on their doors, so the angel passed over. After the last plague, Pharaoh finally allowed the Israelites to leave after much resistance. According to the instructions of Moses, they were to borrow the Egyptians' jewels of silver, jewels of gold, and raiment. It was a mixed multitude that consisted of the Israelites and Egyptians. They also carried flocks, herds, and cattle.

When the Israelites left, God allowed Pharaoh's heart to be hardened. Pharaoh and his servants turned against Israel and decided to go after them. Pharaoh gathered his chariot and his people and went for the Israelites. When the Israelites saw Pharaoh and his people coming, they were scared. "And Moses said unto the people, Fear ye not, stand still, and see the salvation of the Lord, which he will shew to you today: for the Egyptians whom ye have seen today, ye shall see them again no more forever. The Lord shall fight for you, and ye shall hold your peace." Exodus 14: 13-14. The Lord told Moses to lift his rod and stretch over the sea, the sea became divided, and the Israelites walked on dry land. God used a pillar of cloud during the day and a pillar of fire at night to guide his people.

Pharaoh and the Egyptians continued to pursue the Israelites with their chariots. Finally, the wheels fell off, and they decided to return because they said God was with the Israelites and against the Egyptians. Moses outstretched his rod over the sea, and the waters went back and covered Pharaoh and his people. They were drowned, never to bother God's people again. The Israelites walked on dry land. The people saw the power of God. They feared and believed in God and also Moses. God is always there to protect his children from danger. Always pray to God for his guiding care and protection when you feel in danger. He is always there to cover and protect his children. Exodus 12-14. "The angel of the Lord encampeth round about them that fear him, and delivereth them." Psalm 34:7.

Despite the problems you face, however big or small they may be and seem endless, you are never left alone to suffer. The angels of God provide protection and assistance for his children in times of their greatest need. The Lord will never forsake his children who believe in him. Children and teens who seek the help of God during their challenging moments to protect themselves from Satan, in love and mercy, God will fight their battles against the Devil for them. "Touch not mine anointed, and do my prophets no harm." Psalm 105:15

God is very close to children who stand up for him. Jesus connects his interest with those of his faithful children. Jesus suffered for his children, and anyone who tries to hurt them is hurting Jesus. The strength of God is always close to you to deliver you from danger. Because of this, you can stand for Jesus in these situations without following Satan. If anyone tries to fight, tell lies, or do any other evil, you can pray, leave it to God, and walk away. Jesus cares and watches over his children to keep them safe all the time from danger. God sends mighty angels from heaven to protect his children.

Psalm 91 "He that dwelleth in the secret place of the most high shall abide under the shadow of the Almighty. I will say of the Lord He is my refuge and my fortress: my God; in him will I trust. Surely he shall deliver thee from the snare of the fowler and from the noisome pestilence. He shall cover thee with his feathers, and under his wings shalt thou trust: his truth shall be thy shield and buckler. Thou shalt not be afraid for the terror by night; nor for the arrow that flieth by day. Nor for the pestilence that walketh in darkness; nor for the destruction that wasteth at noonday. A thousand shall fall at thy side, and ten thousand at thy right hand, but it shall not come nigh thee. Only with thine eyes shalt thou behold and see the reward of the wicked. Because thou hast made the Lord, which is my refuge, even the most high, thy habitation. There shall no evil befall thee, neither shall any plague come nigh thy dwelling. For he shall give his angels charge over thee, to keep thee in thy ways. They shall bear thee up in their hands, lest thou dash thy foot against a stone. Thou shalt tread upon the lion and adder: the young lion and the dragon shalt thou trample under feet. Because he hath set his love upon me, therefore will I deliver him: I will set him on high because he hath known my name. He shall call upon me, and I will answer him: I will be with him in trouble; I will deliver him and honor him. With long life will I satisfy him, and shew him my salvation."

Kindness

A poor boy sold things to different homes to send himself to school. One day, the boy realized that he only had a dime and was experiencing hunger. The boy decided to ask for food at another home. But when a beautiful young lady opened the door, he became nervous and asked for a glass of water instead of food. She observed that the boy was hungry and gave him a large cup of milk instead of water. He took his time to drink the milk, and after it was finished, he asked the young lady, "How much do I owe you?" She answered, "You do not owe me anything. Mother has taught us to never accept pay for a kindness done."

"Then I thank you from the bottom of my heart," he replied. When Howard Kelly left home, he was not just physically strengthened, but his faith became stronger in God and man. He was prepared to give up on life, but he gained encouragement from that experience. Many years after, the young lady was seriously ill. The doctors in her hometown were troubled and decided to send her to the large city where various specialists were located. These specialists were informed about her rare disease and to study the condition. A request was made for Dr. Howard Kelly to conduct the consultation.

When Dr. Kelly heard about the town that the patient came from, his eyes brightened. Quickly he hurried to the hospital hall to the room of the patient. While Dr. Kelly was dressed in his coat, he looked at the patient and realized immediately who she was. He went back to his office and decided to do all he could to preserve her life.

Since that day, he paid attention to her especially. After a lengthy fight, the battle ended victoriously. The day came when she was to be sent home from the hospital. Dr. Kelly asked the business office to show him the total payment of the hospital bill for his agreement. He observed the bill, made a note on its edge, and delivered it to her room. She was scared to open the bill because she believed her extended hospitalization would take her a lifetime to complete payment. After all, it was expensive. Finally, she opened it because she had been waiting for a long while. The note on the edge of the bill grabbed her attention, and she read the message: "Paid in full with one glass of milk." Dr. Howard Kelly signed. Tears of happiness filled her eyes as her joyful heart prayed to God, "Thank You, God that your love has spread abroad through human hearts and hands." "Be kindly affectionated one to another with brotherly love; in honor preferring one another." Roman 12:10.

Dorcas was a kind woman. She helped the poor and widows where she lived. Dorcas would sew clothing for them and treat them with kindness. She became ill and died. The people with who she showed kindness were really saddened by her death. They laid her in a room. The disciples heard that Peter was there. He was one of Jesus' disciples, and God had given him the blessing of the Holy Spirit. They sent Peter to come and see Dorcas. They took him to the room where she lay dead. The widows were weeping and showing the coats and garments she made for them.

Peter told them to leave the room. He knelt and prayed for her. He told Dorcas to arise, and she opened her eyes. When she saw Peter, she sat up. Peter stretched out his hand and lifted her. He then called the widows and persons she showed kindness to see her. The news spread throughout Joppa, and they believed in the Lord. Acts 9: 36-42. "And be ye kind one to another, tenderhearted, forgiving one another, even as God for Christ's sake hath forgiven you." Ephesians 4: 32.

Kindness should be shown to everyone with who we come in contact. Dorcas made it her duty to sew for the widows and the poor. You can choose some act of kindness to do. It could be your neighbor who needs food, and you have extra that you can share. Children and adolescents should share gifts with children's homes, needy families, the sick, disabled individuals, and the elderly. They can comb the hair of the elderly and persons who are disabled and clean their homes, especially if they have no assistance. You could share your lunch with a classmate who has none. It could be your parent or guardian doing chores to assist them in the home. Acts of kindness can come in several ways. Choose a way to show kindness to others all the time. Jesus is kind to us, so we should be kind to others.

Make the rule of kindness be in your thinking, speech, and actions. It will deliver excellent results. You will be gentle, have good manners and show care to others. These qualities are necessary for your development as children of God. The Holy Spirit acts as the conscience, which are the thoughts that tell you what is right or wrong. When you have the Holy Spirit, he changes your life, and you will not hurt others but care for them. Your face will express the beauty of Jesus. Jesus wants children and teens to be like him.

Jesus Christ will assist his children to have love and to talk gently and kindly to everyone. The grace of God is love that you should not receive because we have evil ways. Because of the grace of God, your lives can be changed from bad behaviors like bad manners, unkind words, and actions to good behaviors. As children of God, we should always express love and kindness to people who are sad. When someone is happy, you should also be satisfied with them. We should always make people happy around us with our kind words and actions. Be a ray of sunshine to others by showing them kindness. Do not be selfish; always seek to help others.

Give, and it will Come Back to You

Give, and it will come back to you,

Good measure pressed down,

Shaken together and running over,

Give, and it will come back to you.

When you give to the Lord,

Give in love, give in faith,

Give with joy and a smile on your face,

Give as the Lord has given to you.

How you give is a reflection of your gratitude,

So give, give to the Lord,

From your heart, give your best,

Give unto God, and you will be blessed.

Do not be stingy; do not be tight,

Learn from the widow in the Bible,

Who gave her the last mite.

People rob God when they do not give tithes and offerings,

And they do not understand why they have been cut off,

From heavenly blessings.

Abundant life and prosperity begin when you,

Prove your love for God by giving to Him.

Obedience

In 1685 Sarah, Abraham LeFevre's wife in France, baked the family Bible in a loaf of bread before the United States of America gained independence from England. What an interesting action! "How could she do something like that?" We pondered. In the 16th and 17th centuries, the LeFevre family were French Protestants known as Huguenots. They had been experiencing freedom for eighty-seven years, thanks to the renowned Edict of Nantes of 1598, which allowed the Huguenots to have worship and church services as they wished.

The Catholic King Louis XIV then abolished the Edict of Nantes on October 18, 1685. As a result, there was turbulent persecution. Nobody was authorized to read the Bible for themselves or even own a volume of the Bible. Huguenots were forbidden from being baptized or teaching their children about their protestant faith. The Huguenots' churches and documents were burned; their property was taken away, and they were banned from leaving the country.

They resided close to Strasbourg in France, the Alsace-Lorraine area, which is situated opposite (across) the Rhine River from Bavaria, Germany. The LeFevre family had a Geneva Bible that was produced in 1608 in the country of Switzerland. The Geneva Bible was smaller and had a greater development than the heavy volumes of the Great Bible and Tyndale versions that came before it. Nevertheless, the Bible was so valuable to the LeFevre family that they did not want anyone to get rid of it.

Abraham and Sarah knew that the French army would thoroughly search their home and possibly be detained and martyred them for their Christian beliefs. How would they be able to keep the family Bible safe? Where could they conceal it so the French army could not find it? Sarah must have been a brave and clever woman. This idea came to her while she was baking bread for the family. No one would examine a loaf of bread large enough to hold the Bible, even if it was evident to them.

Sarah wrapped the precious Bible in vellum (a piece of paper made from animal skin) by putting it in the center of the dough and kneading it perfectly for protection from heat. She left the dough to rise before placing it in the oven for baking, keeping a close eye on it to ensure the loaf did not overbake. She set the golden bread on the table to cool after taking it out of the oven. Father Abraham assembled his six children around the table and warned them to protect the Bible cautiously. They were told to snatch the loaf of bread with the Bible inside and go to the home of Daniel and Marie Ferree, which was close by if anything happened. The Ferree family were wealthy Huguenot neighbors.

Isaac, 16 years old, was not present when the army stormed LeFevre's home and murdered his family members. Can you imagine his anguish when he walked inside his house and saw the bodies of his loved ones? Isaac hastily snatched the large loaf of bread on the table, which contained the Bible, and dashed toward the neighbor's home. While on his way, a soldier stopped him and snatched the loaf from his grip. Isaac's heart was thumping so loudly that he feared the man would notice and grow suspicious. "Rather a heavy loaf you have there, lad." The man hefted it and then flung it back into Isaac's arms. "Here! Take it back. It feels much too doughy for me."

He rushed to the Ferree's home, hugging the loaf. Isaac knocked rapidly, using a pre-programmed signal of two loud and one quiet tap. Daniel gazed into the darkness as the door slowly opened. When he saw Isaac, he dragged the distressed lad inside. "Hurry! We must flee!" Isaac sobbed. "They killed my parents and all my brothers and sisters." During the night, Isaac and the Ferree family sneaked through the darkness carrying their minimal necessities. They ran across the Rhine River into Bavaria, predominantly Lutheran territory. Isaac remained with the Ferree family till 1708. Isaac loved Catherine, who was Ferree's daughter. They got married in 1704, and their first son was born in Germany. Isaac gave his son the name Abraham after his martyred father. "Children, obey your parents in the Lord, for this is right. Honour thy father and mother, which is the first commandment with promise. That it may be well with thee, and thou mayest live long on the Earth." Ephesians 6: 1-3.

When God made man, the Earth was perfect until Adam and Eve sinned. The Earth became sinful and wicked. The heavenly Father saw that every imagination of man's heart was continually evil. God was sorry he had made man. He decided that he would destroy the Earth. "But Noah found grace in the eyes of the Lord." Genesis 6:8. He had three sons; their names were: Shem, Ham, and Japheth. God spoke to Noah and made a covenant to build an ark. He and his family would go into the ark and be saved. God would destroy the Earth because it was corrupt and filled with violence. God told Noah how he should build the ark. Noah obeyed God and built the ark. He told the other people that God would destroy the Earth. They mocked and jeered him. He preached to them while he built the ark. Noah followed God and was obedient to what he told him to do. He was faithful to God; although he had never seen rainfall, he listened to God's instructions. "By faith Noah, being warned of God of things not seen as yet, moved with fear, prepared an ark for the saving of his house; by the which he condemned the world, and became an heir of righteousness which is by faith." Hebrews 11:7.

The day came when Noah, his family, and the animals in pairs and sevens entered the ark. The unclean animals went into the ark as pairs, and the clean ones went in groups of sevens. The people still didn't believe it. When the family of Noah all entered the ark, God closed the door. Then the rain began to fall. The water destroyed everything that was upon the land. Only Noah, his family, and the animals who entered the ark in pairs and groups of sevens were saved. It rained for forty days and nights. Noah never disobeyed God. Genesis 6 - Genesis 10:1. Everything God told him to do, he did, and he and his family were saved. "And this is love, that we walk after his commandments. This is the commandment, that, as ye have heard from the beginning, ye should walk in it." 2 John 1:6.

Children and teenagers should be obedient to their parents, guardians, or those in charge of them in the Lord. We will be saved from many dangers. Some persons would be alive today if they obeyed God or their parents in the Lord. We should always endeavor to be obedient. It will prove a blessing. Sometimes, you might grumble and be upset when asked to do a task. But each small duty or activity is preparing you for bigger ones. If you don't try to be obedient to the small things, you will not be able to manage when the larger ones come.

When children pray in the name of Jesus, He will strongly influence their lives. It means that you must follow His ways, show His love and do the work of God. He says, "If ye love me, keep my commandments." John 14:15. If you love God, you will be obedient to his commandments. Genuine obedience comes from the heart that is connected to Jesus. If you listen to Jesus, He will guide your thoughts and actions. Children who are obedient to Jesus will carry out his work with happiness. When they follow Jesus, they will always obey Him and hate sinful behaviors. Christ was obedient to His heavenly Father, so we are to obey God. If you are determined to be obedient to Jesus, he will give you the strength to obey. He will also make you wise and strong. As long as the family is obedient to God, they will be happy.

Obedience is the Very Best

Obedience is the very best way to show that you believe.

Doing exactly as the Lord commands, doing it happily.

Action is the key, do it immediately, the joy you will receive.

Obedience is the very best way to show that you believe.

O-B-E-D-I-E-N-C-E.

Obedience is the very best way to show that you believe.

We want to live pure, we want to live`clean, we want to do our best.

Sweetly submitting to authority, leaving to God the rest.

Walking in the light, keeping our attitude right, on the narrow way.

For if we believe the Word we receive, we always will obey.

O-B-E-D-I-E-N-C-E.

Obedience is the very best way to show that you believe.

Disobedience

Fourteen-year-old Anusha always cries whenever she talks about her father. Her Father was enraged because she converted to Christianity, and he persuaded her to reconsider her decision. The problem began when a Seventh-day Adventist neighbor told her mother about Jesus Christ. "Idol worship is not right," the neighbor explained. "You should give your heart to Jesus." Mother began attending an Adventist church in her area after listening to her neighbor regularly, who encouraged her to accept Jesus Christ. Anusha accompanied her mother, who seemed to appreciate the singing. Father refused to attend church with Mother and Anusha in the community. He insisted on preventing Mother and Anusha from attending church. He showed them the twenty wooden and stone idols inside their house. "Our gods have helped us for so many years," he said. "Our gods have taken care of us and protected us. Why do you want to go to church to worship another God?"

Mom never answered him. Anusha remained silent during the entire conversation. They couldn't say anything to make Father peaceful. When Father noticed that they continued to attend church, he talked with her mother harshly. Father spanked Anusha for disobedience.

Other neighbors mocked Anusha and Mother, making the situation worse. "You worshipped our gods for so long," said someone. "What went wrong, so you have to worship the Christian God?" The local priest teased them, even though he was not a Christian. Father suffered a severe accident just when it appeared things couldn't get much worse. A truck struck him while riding his bicycle down a busy road. The hospital admitted him in critical condition.

"Only God can save him," the doctor informed Mother. Father's life was in danger, Mother and Anusha prayed to Jesus for help, and the Adventist neighbor prayed. Her dad recuperated and was able to return home after three weeks, much to the amazement of the doctors. Father slowly recognized that the God of the universe had saved his life. But he became furious again and told Mother and Anusha they couldn't go to church anymore. On the Sabbath morning, Mother and Anusha had to hide and leave home for church.

Eventually, Anusha was fortunate to attend an Adventist boarding school for further education. She's happy because she won't be punished or beaten if she worships Jesus. At school, she was given her very own Bible. She reads the Bible to her friends on holiday at home. Anusha taught many of her friends how to pray to the God of heaven. She wants to study the Bible and pray with Dad more than anything else to accept God in his life. Children and teenagers should be obedient to their parents, but if their parents are forcing them to do actions contrary to the Ten Commandments or preventing them from accepting Jesus in their lives, they should disobey them."He that loveth father or mother more than me is not worthy of me." Matthew 10:37.

Laurie and Israel are brothers. They reside in the highlands of Papua New Guinea with their parents. Israel and Laurie are similar to most young boys; they like playing and getting into trouble. During break time, Israel would sneak away from school to play with Laurie, and the boys would hide in the family's garden, searching for ripe bananas to enjoy. They would run away and play if their parents asked them to carry a jug of water from the well, remove the white fleshy fruit from the coconut shells, or do any other chore they refused to do it. Israel and Laurie enjoyed singing about Jesus' love during Sabbath School. Still, it was sometimes difficult for them to realize that following the instructions of mother and father was just as necessary as being obedient to God. The parents disciplined the boys whenever they were misbehaving or disobedient. The boys would regret it, but recalling to be obedient was difficult.

Israel and Laurie were playing outside their home one day. They had constructed mock trucks and buses out of sticks and fruits. They took small, firm round fruits and inserted a short stick between two of them to create the wheels and axle of the truck. They then divided a longer stick and tied it around the truck's axle. The longer stick turned into a handle. The boys were having a good time running about their yard with their stick trucks, making truck noises while they moved. Immediately, Laurie was startled to notice a brilliant light behind his elder brother. Laurie had to shield his eyes from the light, which was brighter than the midday sunlight. Laurie took a deep breath and remained completely still. "Israel, there's an angel standing behind you!" He exclaimed with his eyes widening. Israel's eyes got larger as he raised his head. He, too, noticed an angel standing behind Laurie. As if to protect Laurie, the angel extended his wings. "Laurie, there's an angel behind you, too!"

Israel exclaimed as he leaped to his feet. The boys stood still, making sure not to move, gazing at the angels. The angels were not grumpy or unhappy when they looked at the boys; instead, they were smiling. The boys were not scared, but they remained silent. They simply looked in amazement at the scene in front of them. As if somebody had yelled, the siblings then turned and hurriedly ran to their home to inform their parents what they had witnessed. "Mommy, Daddy, come quick! Our angels are standing outside! We saw our angels!" The parents smiled at their boys and stated, "The angels probably were watching you while you were playing. Perhaps, God has sent the angels to tell you that He is taking care of you, and that He loves you. Even if you don't see your angels, they are watching you."

The children returned to the front door of the house running, only to discover that the brilliant angels had vanished. Only the sunshine of the day lightens the front yard. Israel and Laurie became different children after that day. They usually fight and say hurtful things to each other. However, they don't say evil things to one another; if they are tempted to fight, they always recall their angels looking.

Israel and Laurie are still prone to forgetting what their parents have asked them to do. Since that day, Israel and Laurie had seen their very own angels; their mother and father have noticed a difference in their lives.

Israel enjoys sharing testimony with his friends about the day he witnessed his angel. When he gives his testimony, he informs them, "Angels take care of us. They show us that God loves us." Boys and girls, each one of us has an angel to watch over us and protect us, just as Israel's and Laurie's angels do. You may never see your angel, but you can be sure that he is there because the Bible tells us, "He shall give His angels charge over you, to keep you in all your ways." Psalm. 91:11, NKJV.

The Israelites were getting near the Promised Land, but the other nations were an obstacle in their way. The king of Moab, Balak, saw how Israel had defeated the Amorites. He feared them because they were many, and the Moabites couldn't overpower them. So Balak wanted a curse to come upon the Israelites. He heard of Balaam, how whatever he blessed was blessed and what he cursed was cursed. So he decided to send his servants with gifts for Balaam so he would curse Israel. The king also wanted to see him.

The king sent more gifts to Balaam, and he decided to go to the king with the king's princes of Moab. God was angry with the decision he made. He rode on a donkey to see the king. While riding, the angel of the Lord stood in the donkey's way. When the donkey saw the angel, he went into the field and beat the donkey to turn the right way. The donkey thrust himself into the wall, and the foot of Balaam crushed. He was still hitting the donkey. The angel stood in the way that he could not go left or right, and the donkey fell under Balaam. "For we ourselves also were sometimes foolish, disobedient, deceived, serving divers lusts and pleasures, living in malice and envy, hateful, and hating one another." Titus 3: 3.

The Lord opened the donkey's mouth and asked Balaam why he was beating him. Balaam told the donkey that he mocked him. The donkey said to him that he had never disobeyed him. His eyes became open, and he saw the angel of the Lord standing. The angel told him that he would have killed him if it was not for the donkey. The angel told him that he should continue his journey but only speak what God says when he goes to the king. When he went to the king, each time he was to curse Israel, he blessed the nation, and the king was displeased. Numbers 22-23. "And the Lord saith, because they have forsaken my law which I set before them, and have not obeyed my voice, neither walked therein, but have walked after the imagination of their own heart, and after Baalim, which their fathers taught them :Therefore thus saith the Lord of hosts, the God of Israel; Behold, I will feed them, even this people, with wormwood, and give them water of gall to drink." Jeremiah 9:13-15.

It is always best to obey God whatever God wants us to do, we should obey him. He gave his ten commandments to guide us when we make our decisions. We should never be disobedient to God and the prompting of the conscience. When Jesus left the Earth, he left the Holy Spirit with us. The Holy Spirit works on our conscience to make the right decisions. We should never forsake and ignore the prompting of the Holy Spirit. If we eat the diet God ordained for us to eat, he will be able to work on our minds. We can be obedient and do the right things.

The first family on Earth was Adam and Eve. They were always happy as long as they obeyed God. When they disobeyed God, Adam and Eve started to misbehave in their home and became unhappy. God ran them out of the Garden of Eden because they were disobedient. They lost their beautiful home. The little acts will increase to bigger ones, so be careful what you do. When you are disobedient to God, He is displeased with your action. When you continue to have bad behaviors and do not stop doing the wrong, you will do even more, leading to criminal activities. God will bless his obedient children. Crime and violence filled the world because of disobedience. When people introduce you to illegal activities, please do not follow them. Try your best to obey God and live by His commandments with His help.

Cooperation

Cooperation is a big word and so is obedience,

But when I do what the papa says, do what the mama says,

It seems to make a big difference.

My mama teaches me cooperation,

She says I'm old enough to lend her a hand,

So I pick up all my toys, I don't make too much noise,

I think I'm doing all that I can!

Cooperation is a big word and so is obedience,

But when I do what my papa says, do what my mama says,

It seems to make a big difference.

Cause if I'm nasty to my mother,

And if I don't listen to my dad,

They will choose to remind me of the parts that're behind me,

And I tell them that it feels pretty bad.

Cooperation is a big word and so is obedience,

But when you do what your papa says, do what your mama says,

I tell you, oh, the pain, it prevents.

But I like helping my mother,

And I like minding my dad,

Cause when I'm good, and they know it,

Their faces will show it, and it always makes me feel very glad.

And if I go and do a bad thing,

I'm feeling both sick and upset,

I just say I'm sorry, don't fret, don't worry,

My Jesus, he forgives and forgets.

Cooperation is a big word so is obedience,

But when I do what my Jesus says, do what my parents say,

It seems to make a big difference!

Friendship

A wealthy man sat in his magnificent home in Switzerland one morning. He was sad and lonely. He didn't have any friends with whom he could share his concerns. So he knelt alone, pleading with God to send him a friend. On the same morning and in the same town, a young boy learned of Jesus' second coming. His heart swelled with happiness at the promise of seeing his Savior soon. He yearned to share this truth with others so that they, too, may experience the same joy.

He had decided to share a book about Christ's second coming with others door to door. He prayed before leaving his room that morning that God would lead him to individuals who needed assistance. The boy offered a prayer to God to send an angel ahead of him to prepare people to purchase the book. This boy traveled everywhere on the city streets, showing people his book, talking to them about Jesus Christ, and getting orders meanwhile. As a result, the morning flew by until it was almost afternoon. There were still a few homes left on the street where the boy was conducting his work, for he hadn't contacted yet. Before stopping for lunch, he intended to finish his work on that street.

The next home was spacious and lovely. He feared calling on such wealthy individuals since they regularly refused to let him in. Nevertheless, he ought not to skip any of the homes. He stepped towards the door and wiped his feet on the large rug before re-wiping them. The boy rang the doorbell of the wealthy man's house. Then he stopped and waited. A servant soon opened the door, and the boy handed him his business card. The servant brought the business card to his master. He reappeared after a few moments. "The master is at lunch," he explained. "He is sure you have nothing that will interest him, and he does not wish to be disturbed."

"Thank you," the lad replied and then walked away from the house.

He heard someone hurrying after him just a few moments later. When he turned around, he saw the servant he had just left. "The master wishes you to return at once if you are so kind," he remarked. The young man hurried back to the wealthy mansion where he encountered a charming, old Swiss gentleman. The gentleman led the young man into the dining room, seated him at the table, and instructed the servant to place a plate on the table. The boy and the gentleman were soon left alone.

"My boy," stated the gentleman, "This morning, I prayed to God to send me a friend. I was lonely and discouraged, and I knew no one to whom I cared to turn. Just now, when I sent you away, a voice told me distinctly, ''There I sent you a friend, and you have sent him away!' So I called you back. Now, why did God send you to me? What have you brought me?"

The boy's heart swelled with tenderness towards this man. The man had everything money could purchase, yet he was unaware of the hope of Jesus' second coming. The young man looked at the man with promise and happiness in his eyes, which he had discovered in following the precepts of the Lord.

"I have brought you a book which contains a message of hope and courage and faith in the friend of friends, who can give you all that you wish," the young man responded.

The man was fascinated. His heart began to swell with hope, and he believed that God had sent this young man in response to his prayer. He offered the young man to come to his house and study the Bible with him every week. God is searching for the sincere, praying ones and preparing them for Jesus Christ second coming. "A man that hath friends must shew himself friendly: and there is a friend that sticketh closer than a brother." Proverbs 18: 24.

Martha, Mary, and Lazarus were siblings. The Heavenly Father sent his Son Jesus Christ into this sinful world to die for mankind. While he was on Earth, he had no place to call home. Jesus went to the home of Lazarus and his siblings' home regularly. When he wanted to rest or eat some food, he would go to Martha's house. She took care of him, and the siblings loved Jesus. He healed the sick and did many miracles; he even raised Lazarus to life. One day, he was having a feast with the Pharisees. Mary came behind him weeping. While he was around the table, she bent down and used her tears to wash his feet, her hair to dry his feet, and kissed his feet. Mary bought an alabaster box of ointment. She also anointed his feet with the expensive ointment she purchased. Jesus told her she had many sins, and he had forgiven her. John 12, Luke 7: 36-50. The faith of Mary had saved her, and she should go in peace. "Greater love hath no man than this, that a man lay down his life for his friends." John 15:13.

We should foster good friendships with people. Sometimes, when no one can assist you, a friend can help you with your challenges. You might not have friendships with everyone. If you find someone like you or a group of individuals, who share similar values and beliefs, you can befriend and support each other. It is good to have a good relationship with people. Always try to look for the good in others, they might not share your beliefs or values, but you can still relate to them. Friendship helps us to groom and find ourselves in society. You might not know everything, but a friend can share an idea and show you something you never knew. God wants to befriend our fellow men. Jesus' friends were his disciples, and he had some he was closer to than others. He would speak to his friends when he wanted to eat or with someone to talk to.

My friend, do you Love Jesus?

My friend, do you love Jesus?

Oh yes, I love Jesus!

Are you sure you love Jesus?

I'm sure I love Jesus!

And why do you love Jesus?

That's why I love Jesus:

Because He first loved me!

(That's the reason we all ought to love Him)

Oh, how I love Jesus!

Oh, how I love Jesus!

Oh, how I love Jesus!

Because he first loved me!

Happiness

The elderly gentleman walked gently into the restaurant. He leaned on his faithful cane with each slow step, his head tilted, and his shoulders bowed forward. He stood out from the regular Sunday morning breakfast crowd with his ragged cloth jacket, patched pants, worn-out shoes, and pleasant personality. She will never forget his pale blue eyes that shone similar to diamonds, big pink cheeks, and thin lips clasped in a tight and unwavering smile. He came to a complete stop, looked around, and smiled at a small girl sitting near the restaurant's door. She returned his smile with a huge one of her own. Mary observed him hobbling towards a table that was close to the window.

Mary dashed to where he was and stated, "Here, Sir. Let me give you a hand with that chair." He smiled and nodded a thank you without saying anything. She drew away a chair from the table in the restaurant. She supported him with one arm as he moved in front of the chair and sat comfortably. She then pushed the table closer to him and placed his cane against it to reach it. In a gentle clear voice, he remarked, "Thank you, Miss. And bless you for your kind gestures."

"You are welcome, Sir," she answered. "My name is Mary. I will be back in a moment, but if you need anything else in the meantime, just wave at me!"

Mary gave him the change from his ticket after he had a delicious meal of pancakes and hot lemon tea. He just left the money there. She assisted him in getting out from behind the table and out of his chair. She took his cane from him and guided him to the restaurant's front door. Mary opened the door for the elderly man and said, "Come back and see us, Sir!" He turned with his whole body, winked a smile, and nodded a thank you. "You are very kind," he said gently. Mary was on the verge of passing out when she wiped his table.

She discovered a business card and a note written on a napkin. The man hid one hundred dollars underneath the napkin.

The writing on the napkin stated: "Dear Mary, I respect you very much, and you respect yourself too. It shows by the way you treat others. You have found the secret of happiness. Your kind gestures will shine through those who meet you." The old man for whom she had waited so patiently was the restaurant owner where she was employed. It was the first time she or any of his employees had seen him personally. "Happy is he that hath the God of Jacob for his help, whose hope is in the Lord his God." Psalm 146: 5.

Abram and Sarai were an elderly couple. They wanted a child but never had any. The Lord appeared to Abram at the age of ninety-nine years, and his wife was ninety years old. The Lord told him he and his wife would have a son; his name would be Isaac. When God told him, he laughed. God said that Abram would be a father of many nations. God told him he would bless Sarai; she would be a mother of many nations. God changed his name from Abram to Abraham and his wife Sarai to Sarah. When she heard that she would have a son, Sarai laughed but later denied that she laughed. God told her there was nothing too hard for him to do. Sarah later conceived, and Isaac was born. They both laughed, but God fulfilled his promise, and both were happy to have their son. Genesis 17:18-21. "Happy is that people, that is in such a case: yea, happy is that people, whose God is the Lord." Psalm 144:15.

They have lived so long without having a child; God blessed them and made them happy. God wants us to be happy people. If we follow him, he will also bring happiness to us. People are so glad for many things, getting married, eating their favorite meal, finding a true friend, and getting good grades in school or a test. Finding a long-lost friend or relative, getting a home, buying a new car, playing a favorite game with friends who you love, going to church or a place of entertainment, seeing your parents, guardian, or someone who cares for you come home. There are so many situations that make us happy. We should try to maintain happiness even when we are not having our favorite moments. We should always try to be happy by being thankful and having a spirit of gratitude.

When you share the light of Jesus with others, it reflects on you as well. Each act of kindness to a sad soul and needy individual will be a blessing to the giving person. The good you do for others will make you feel better physically and mentally. Even when you are sick, you should be happy; this can make you get better quickly. Jesus wants his children to be happy at all times. Happiness should not be of ourselves but because of Jesus. We should be thankful each day for the blessings of the Lord. We should praise him each day for his loving care, which will make us happy, and we will be able to cope with life's challenges. You should always be cheerful despite the struggles in life. The Lord brings disappointments and trials to expose our sinful behaviors. Sin brings unhappiness, but when we live for Jesus, it brings happiness.

Happiness is to know the Savior

Happiness is to know the savior,

Living a life in His favor,

Having a change in my behavior,

Happiness is the Lord.

Happiness is a new creation,

Jesus and I, in a close relation,

Having a part in His salvation,

Happiness is the Lord.

Real joy is mine,

No matter if the teardrops start,

I've found a secret,

It's Jesus in my heart.

Happiness is to be forgiven,

Living a life that's worth living,

Taking a try that leads to Heaven,

Happiness is the Lord.

Real joy is mine,

No matter if the teardrops start,

I've found a secret,

It's Jesus in my heart,

Jesus in my heart.

Happiness is to be forgiven,

Living a life that's worth living,

Taking a trip that leads to Heaven,

Happiness is the Lord,

Happiness is the Lord.

Depression

She turned her journal's pages, filled with gloomy writing and depressive thinking. She took a sheet of paper and started writing. More sad thoughts poured out onto the page. What's the point? She thought. Nothing that she did make her joyful, not even for a moment. Death would be much easier than fighting against this sadness. But then a new thought occurred to her: death is for a person who does not have any strength. She struggled to keep her composure. It took all the energy she had just to get to her class.

Vasily (vah-SEE-lee) attended a university in Tomsk (tom'sk), Siberia. She lived a double life for a long while. Almost everyone thought of her as a compassionate and reliable person, involved in sports, and a great student. However, she was depressed and felt lonely. She used alcohol and then drugs attempting to get rid of her depression. She could hardly keep her grades up and concealed her addictions and depression from her relatives, but it was challenging. Whenever Vasily mustered the courage to pull herself out of bed every day, she found herself again saying that she wanted the depression to end.

"Good morning," Galina, the lady who cleans the floor, spoke with a smile.

"Morning," She grumbled, thinking that the cleaner lady was even more joyful than her.

She was even joyful when cleaning the dirty toilets. She always made friends with the students, and several students told her about their challenges. She knew the cleaner lady was a Christian because she listened to her speaking to them about God. "Why can't I be happy like Galina?" She murmured to herself.

Galina gave her a Bible as a present and lent her a few books to read one day. She wasn't paying attention to her classwork, so instead of studying, she read books from the cleaner lady. She attempted to read the Bible but felt frustrated and put it down. Vasily returned the books and avoided her. Her depression became worse, and her crazy behavior became more frequent. Her perplexed parents were at a loss for what they could do. Finally, she quit consuming alcohol and using drugs and felt a lot better. However, the depression still was on her. Suicidal thoughts were close to her. It appeared to be the only way out on some days.

She recalled Galina, who might be able to assist her. After some time, she encountered her in the hall. Galina gave her an invitation to come to her home that same afternoon. She accepted but was surprised by her invitation's timing. She recognized that Galina's invitation was not ordinary, but God sanctioned it. God hasn't abandoned what she was thinking; as she approached Galina's house, her heartfelt nearly light. When they spoke, she recognized that God gave Galina a message to give her. Vasily welcomed Jesus to be always a part of her life with the assistance of Galina. When Galina offered a prayer for her, she felt joyful at that moment for many years for the first.

Galina gave her an invitation to attend church, and she accepted. Vasily found happiness in prayer and bible study. Although her sadness had not completely vanished, she knew God was fighting her battle. She does not want to die anymore; instead, she desires to live and share the joy of living with Jesus Christ with people. Vasily's parents believed that she was gone crazy when she informed them of her decision to follow Jesus Christ. However, as they observed the improvements in her attitude, they recognized that God was present in her life and that she was doing much better. Her mother started reading the Bible to see what she was discovering. She even accompanied her to the Seventh-Day Adventist church. Vasily's father regarded her beliefs and accepted what God was doing in his daughter's life. She was eager to share what God was doing in her life with everyone she encountered.

When she returned to school, she could concentrate on her schoolwork. Her grades have improved, and she is more driven than ever to achieve to the best of her ability. She was still experiencing challenges, but God was with her and guided her through them. Whenever she realizes her depression, she knows God will pick her up and bring her through the difficult moments. People used to believe that she was the family's black sheep. However, now she is God's precious lamb, following Jesus Christ, her gentle Shepherd.

"Fear thou not; for I am with thee: be not dismayed; for I am thy God: I will strengthen thee; yea, I will help thee; yea, I will uphold thee with the right hand of my righteousness." Isaiah 41:10.

Elijah was a prophet of God, and his lifestyle pleased God. There was a famine in Israel and the surrounding nations for three years. God commanded him to prove to the people who was the true God. He asked the prophets of Baal to make an altar to their God, and he made an altar to God. They were to call upon their god named Baal for fire to come from heaven and burn their sacrifice. They cried all day to their god, but no fire came. Elijah cried to God, and fire came from heaven and burned up everything, including that water poured on the altar. After the fire, the rain also came from heaven.

Ahab and Jezebel were rulers, and when Jezebel heard, she threatened to kill Elijah. Elijah was so afraid that he ran into the wilderness to hide and sat under a tree. He requested God to take his life. He was so depressed and wanted to die. An angel came to him twice while he was sleeping under the tree. The angel awakened him and gave him a cake to eat and water to drink twice. The Lord then appeared to him. He heard the wind, felt the earthquake, and saw the fire, but God was not in them. God approached him in a still, small voice. He told the Lord how he felt. Elijah was depressed and believed he couldn't manage anymore. The Lord didn't allow him to die. But he was translated in a chariot of fire to be with God. 1 Kings 18-2 Kings 2. "Casting all your care upon him; for he careth for you." I Peter 5:7.

Sometimes, you might experience feelings of giving up because of the circumstances you are going through. You might have suicidal thoughts that are plaguing your mind. Trials that seem so impossible that you see no way of recovering from them. Impending doom, hopeless, helpless, and unable to cope with life challenges. You question your belief in God, want to give up God, and no longer want to believe in God. There is nobody to turn to for assistance. Everywhere, you may see a dead end. But remember, God cares for you. He loves you with an everlasting love that no man can love you.

The trials you go through will make you stronger when you overcome them. It is a stepping stone for another stage in your life. If you have not gone through it, the blessings that await you might never be fulfilled, or you will not enjoy them. Each person's struggle is different, but God is there for everyone. Reach out to Jesus because he is reaching out to you. Read God's word, the Bible; it is like medicine to your soul. Pray regularly; it isn't necessarily kneeling to pray but just uttering a word God understands. "Pray without ceasing." 1 Thessalonians 5:17.

Read inspirational books and watch inspirational programs that can uplift your spirit. Always know that you might feel this way now, but God has a better plan. It will be as if it is unending, and there is no light at the end of the journey. Just keep holding on, and he will work on what is best for you. "He will never leave you or forsake you." Hebrews 13:5. If there is no one to speak to, relate to God, and he will hear and answer your prayers. The answer might not be the way you want it, but it is what is good for you. Trust in him, believe, and he will surely make a way. "And we know that all things work together for good to them that love God to them who are called according to his purpose." Romans 8:28.

A happy mind is good for the health of the brain and body. Unhappiness will cause children to become sick. Children and teenagers should closely relate to God to be happy individuals. Healthy Christian children and teenagers should encourage sick people to trust God and be cheerful. Cheerfulness and trust in God will give sick children and teens a chance to get well more quickly. Overcoming sadness will help keep children and teenagers healthy; they will relate to people acceptably and won't show unruly behavior. One of the most important ways to overcome sadness and illness is by showing kindness to others and helping those in need more than themselves. Children and adolescents should express happiness in their faces and their actions.

Boys and girls will face challenging experiences in life, but they are not alone; they are to pray to Jesus in faith to help them to cope with their trials and for him to solve their problems. They should develop a close relationship with Jesus by praying and reading the Bible regularly so that God will guide their lives. No matter how difficult the problems that children face, Jesus will help them because he loves and cares for each boy or girl. Children and adolescents should learn that their challenges can be a blessing in their lives once they are in a loving relationship with Jesus. They should praise and thank God for what he is doing in their lives and will continue to do. Regardless of the difficult circumstances they face or will face, they should always be cheerful even when God does not answer their prayers immediately. However painful your situations may be, boys and girls, Jesus will never leave you; he is beside you; just lift your thoughts to him in prayer.

With Christ in the Vessel

With Christ in the vessel,

We can smile at the storm;

Smile at the storm,

Smile at the storm.

With Christ in the vessel,

We can smile at the storm;

As we go sailing home,

Sailing, sailing home,

Sailing, sailing home.

With Christ in the vessel,

We can smile at the storm;

As we go sailing home.

Patience

A poor Christian man was dying in a small home in France. He called his only child to talk to him; he explained, "My dear little Pierre, you will soon be left alone, and many troubles will come to you in this world, but always remember that all comes from above; then you will find it easy to bear everything with patience." Unfortunately, the needy man died not long after, and young Pierre was left lonely in the world to live. He had no other option except to beg for his livelihood. He would sing for persons as he traveled to different homes in the communities, getting from them just a sufficient amount of money to barely survive. Each time someone gave him money or food, he would comment, "It comes from above," Recalling his father's final words. He made it a custom to speak these words no matter what occurred to him, and he discovered that they did assist him in enduring each situation patiently.

He was going through a community one day when an unexpected blast of wind swept a tile off the roof of a house close by. Pierre was hit on his shoulder, pushing him to the ground. "It comes from above," he said as he regained his footing. However, as you can expect, the individuals standing around burst out laughing. However, a short time later, another burst of wind ripped the entire roof off of a house a little further down the road. It would have slain young Pierre if he continued the journey. As a result, he concluded that the tile that had struck and injured him had truly "came from above."

Another time, a rich man hired young Pierre to deliver an important message to a merchant in a neighboring city. The man instructed Pierre to move quickly; he ran as swiftly as possible. He attempted to jump across a stream when he came to a stream, but he fell in and almost drowned. When he eventually made it to the bank, damp and exhausted, he discovered that the valuable letter had vanished. He looked everywhere but couldn't find anything in the dirty water.

"It comes from above," he mumbled to himself as he painfully made his way back to the rich man's home. Naturally, the man was upset with him. He drove him away from his home. On the other hand, Pierre could only remark, "It comes from above."

The man called for him the following day. "Your falling into that stream was a fortunate accident for me; circumstances have changed overnight. If that letter had been delivered, I would have been involved in serious loss. Please accept this little gift as a token of my gratitude." The man placed some more money in Pierre's small hands; he had not seen this amount of money for a long while. "It comes from above," he remarked while walking down the steps with a smile on his face.

As a result, Pierre grew up knowing that God was organizing his life, confidently expressing that, as Romans 8:28 says, "All things work together for good to them that love God." He later became a successful businessman himself. We should have that kind of faith and patience in God as well. This will save us a lot of unnecessary grief and despair, which fill our minds with tranquility and trust to bear everything patiently as we recall that "all comes from above." "But they that wait upon the Lord shall renew their strength; they shall mount up with wings as eagles; they shall run, and not be weary; and they shall walk, and not faint." Isaiah 40: 31.

God made a promise that he would send his son Jesus to save his children from their sins. Simeon was getting old; he had heard about Jesus' coming and lived a righteous life before God. Finally, the Holy Spirit appeared to him and told Simeon that he would see Jesus before dying. He was an elderly man; he waited patiently to see Jesus when he was born. After Jesus was born, Mary and Joseph carried him to the temple according to the custom of the law.

The Holy Spirit came to Simeon and told him Jesus was in the temple. He went to the temple and saw Jesus with his parents. Simeon took the child in his hands and blessed God. He said he could die in peace because he had seen that God had sent Jesus Christ, His Son to save his people from their sins. Jesus' parents were shocked; he blessed them and told them that Jesus would die. Anna was in the temple, often fasting and praying. She was eighty-four years old. She had come to see Jesus as well. She also waited to see the Savior. She gave thanks to God that Jesus came into this world. They both waited patiently to see Jesus. They were happy to see Jesus. Luke 2: 22-38. "I waited patiently for the Lord; he inclined unto me and heard my cry." Psalm 40:1.

Waiting may seem a very long process, and sometimes, you wait until you never get through. You probably encounter temptations by someone who you can't wait to stop bothering you. The family you're living with, parents or guardians might mistreat you and be abusive. You want something you desire; it could be better food, better living conditions, better health, and even better life. Life is filled with trials and challenges. Pray and wait on God for him to make a way for you. God will answer you, yes, no, or wait. "Wait on the Lord: be of good courage, and he shall strengthen thine heart: wait, I say, on the Lord." Psalm 27:14. Waiting can bring you beautiful results. Many times if you just waited, it would be better for you. It always seems a long process, but be patient. You should exercise patience with the person God places in your life. Patience is a virtue everyone should have.

When going through difficult situations, do not be bothered and remain peaceful. You are not to complain, murmur, be angry and become miserable. Do not do things to hurt yourself or others. The trials of life are to make you become better children and adolescents. Children and adolescents should not make the difficulties they face make them sad. Remain calm and trust the Lord to give you the strength to cope with these situations. You should be happy despite the challenges that you are going through because you are bearing them for the cause of Jesus. Children need to be patient. It will make them better citizens in the world and help them to receive eternal life.

They That Wait Upon the Lord

They that wait upon the Lord shall renew their strength,

They shall mount up with wings like eagles,

They shall run and not be weary,

They shall walk and not faint.

Teach me, Lord; Teach me, Lord,

How to wait.

Bibliography

1. Adventist Mission. (2022). World Mission. No school on Sabbath. https://am.adventistmission.org/mqc19q2-5935

2. Adventist Mission. (2022). World Mission. Shy amazon girl. https://am.adventistmission.org/mqc19q2-5931

3. Adventist Mission. (2022). World Mission. Tragedy opens church. https://am.adventistmission.org/mqc19q2-5937

4. Adventist Mission. (2022). World Mission. God gave me life. https://am.adventistmission.org/mqc19q1-5925

5. Adventist Mission. (2022). World Mission. Singing for daddy. https://am.adventistmission.org/mqc19q2-5930

6. Adventist Mission. (2022). World Mission. Out of the darkness. Retrieved from https://am.adventistmission.org/1207-russia

7. White, E.G. (2022). The Ministry of Healing. The Ministry of Healing — Ellen G. White Writings (egwwritings.org) 237,252

8. Bender, B. (2020, March 6). Steps to Life. Manna from Heaven. https://www.stepstolife.org/article/childrens-story-manna-from-heaven/

9. Songlyrics. Jeff & Sheri Easter - Thank You, Lord, for Your Blessings Lyrics. Retrieved 2022 http://www.songlyrics.com/jeff-sheri-easter/thank-you-lord-for-your-blessings-lyrics/

10. Conti, A. (September 15, 2016). Nuggets of faith mined from the lives of my pioneer missionary family in Alaska, that inspire my life and writing. Bible baked in a loaf of bread. https://annaleeconti.blogspot.com/2016/09/the-bible-baked-in-loaf-of-bread.html

11. Flaslyrics. Peacespeaker. Retrieved December 28, 2022 https:/0/www.flashlyrics.com/lyrics/heritage-singers/peacespeaker-91

12. Flashlyrics. Happiness is to know the saviour. Retrieved December 28, 2022 https://www.flashlyrics.com/lyrics/heritage-singers/happiness-is-the-lord-20

13. Genius. Find us faithful. Retrieved December 28, 2022 https://genius.com/Steve-green-find-us-faithful-lyrics

14. Gospel Choruses and Songs. Around the walls of Jericho. Retrieved December 28, 2022 https://gospelchoruses.wordpress.com/2015/01/10/around-the-walls-of-jericho/

15. Gospel Choruses and Songs. Fill my cup let it overflow. Retrieved December 28, 2022 https://gospelchoruses.wordpress.com/2015/01/24/fill-my-cup-let-it-overflow-with-love/

16. Gospel Choruses and Songs. Heavenly sunshine. Retrieved from December 28, 2022 https://gospelchoruses.wordpress.com/2015/02/04/heavenly-sunshine/

17. Gospel Choruses and Songs. They that wait upon the lord. Retrieved December 28, 2022 https://gospelchoruses.wordpress.com/2014/12/06/they-that-wait-upon-the-lord/

18. How We Tell Time Using the Sun. Retrieved February 6, 2023 https://learning-center.homesciencetools.com/article/how-we-tell-time-using-the-sun/

19. Lynette, G. (August 8, 2018). Steps to Life. Send me a friend. https://www.stepstolife.org/article/childrens-story-send-me-a-friend/

20. Malvina Reynolds: Song Lyrics and Poems. Magic penny. Retrieved from December 28, 2022 https://people.wku.edu/charles.smith/MALVINA/mr101.htm

21. Morgan, C. (2022). Lifehack. Learn the different types of love. https://www.lifehack.org/816195/types-of-love

22. Mission. (2022). News. Finnish Father's Forgiveness Transforms Lives. https://www.adventistmission.org/finnish-fathers-forgiveness-transforms-lives

23. Prayer. The Lords prayer. Retrieved December 28, 2022 https://www.beliefnet.com/prayers/catholic/childrens-prayers/the-lords-prayer.aspx

24. Restoring the Temple – Sunlight: Another Perspective. https://www.stepstolife.org/article/restoring-the-temple-sunlight-another-perspective/

25. Songlyrics. Cooperation. Retrieved December 28, 2022 .http://www.songlyrics.com/the-king-s-heralds/cooperation-lyrics/

26. Steps to Life: A glass of milk. (2020, February 26). https://www.stepstolife.org/article/childrens-story-a-glass-of-milk-2/

27. Steps to Life. Andy's Hands. (2020, March 10). https://www.stepstolife..org/article/childrens-story-andys-hands/

28. Steps to Life. Secret of happiness. (2019, October 18). https://www.stepstolife.org/article/childrens-story-the-secret-of-happiness/

29. Steps to life. The Prayer and Faith of a Little Girl. (2019, June 6). https://www.stepstolife.org/article/childrens-story-the-prayer-and-faith-of-a-little-girl/

30. Stoeckert, K. (2018, March 12). Steps to Life. Never give up.
    https://www.stepstolife.org/article/childrens-story-never-give-up/

31. Timeless Truths. Little feet, be careful. Retrieved December 28,2022
    https://library.timelesstruths.org/music/Little_Feet_Be_Careful/

32. White, E. G. (July 31, 2020). Steps to Life. Keeper of the light.
    https://www.stepstolife.org/article/childrens-story-keeper-of-the-light/

33. White, E. G. (2022). Temperance. https://m.egwwritings.org/en/book/110.926#927

34. White, E. G. (2022). Education. https://m.egwwritings.org/en/book/29.1061#1061

35. White, E. G. (October 23, 2018). Steps to Life. Diet in childhood.
    https://www.stepstolife.org/article/restoring-the-temple-diet-in-childhood/

36. Wagne, J. (2018, March 7). Steps to Life. Kindness repaid
    https://www.stepstolife.org/article/childrens-story-kindness-repaid/

37. WaytoChurch.com. Give and it will come back to you. Retrieved December 8, 2022
    https://waytochurch.com/lyrics/song/11138/give-and-it-will-come-back-to-you

38. WaytoChurch.com. Obedience is the very best. Retrieved December 28. 2022
    https://waytochurch.com/lyrics/song/1850/obedience-is-the-very-best-

39. White, E. G. (2021). Child guidance. https://m.egwwritings.org/en/book/8.1773#1778

40. Retrieved from https://www.Britannica.com, https://www.Scientificamerican.com

41. Retrieved from https://www.esquire.com, https://www.wfmz.com

42. Retrieved from https://www.mallardlawfrim.com, https://www.lawinsider.com

Ann is a pseudonym.

Pictures from www.freepik.com

Activities for Children

S	R	N	U	T	R	I	T	I	O	N	G	J	K	Y	D
G	I	S	K	R	H	G	O	D	D	Z	T	O	T	I	W
S	W	G	L	F	T	B	R	O	E	P	E	Y	E	C	S
C	A	F	S	A	B	B	A	T	H	C	M	T	U	S	A
H	T	H	R	I	D	R	A	F	I	H	P	G	R	F	B
O	E	Z	F	P	K	E	C	F	S	T	E	R	A	C	A
O	R	O	E	X	E	R	C	I	S	E	R	O	N	I	A
L	G	E	L	J	E	R	B	D	M	E	A	W	R	T	L
S	I	G	S	U	N	D	I	A	L	G	N	T	Z	E	H
J	B	Y	T	T	D	M	C	F	E	T	C	P	F	P	A
U	P	J	E	S	U	S	W	A	S	H	E	E	R	T	P
D	T	S	U	N	L	I	G	H	T	W	T	Z	W	T	P
A	O	T	R	U	S	T	I	N	G	O	D	Q	O	R	Y
H	D	T	Z	R	S	W	T	Z	Q	H	Z	K	C	A	W
I	J	F	A	I	T	H	F	U	L	Q	Z	K	C	E	A
T	S	S	I	N	G	I	N	G	B	T	W	E	Q	H	X

Nutrition	Trust in God	Faithful
Diet	Sabbath	Sun dial
Exercise	Heart	Jesus wash
Water	God	Happy
Sunlight	Singing	Judah
Temperance	School	

Puzzle

A	E	J	E	R	U	S	A	L	E	M	S	F	G	Y	T
M	C	U	F	I	S	S	O	F	E	I	S	L	L	E	W
B	V	P	Z	B	R	O	B	E	C	A	V	E	F	A	P
U	F	F	M	I	D	N	I	G	H	T	M	V	L	X	I
I	J	L	E	D	I	R	Y	F	I	G	B	L	K	T	P
L	O	M	O	U	T	H	F	H	R	V	S	K	T	A	L
D	S	E	A	A	T	M	R	R	I	B	T	Y	U	I	O
E	H	R	P	L	T	H	T	H	G	N	R	L	G	P	O
R	U	E	J	E	R	I	C	H	O	F	E	H	S	T	E
S	A	N	I	X	P	E	Q	R	T	M	T	P	T	S	L
T	L	T	R	U	M	P	E	T	L	S	C	K	X	H	I
S	E	A	D	T	V	F	D	K	X	Y	H	R	I	C	S
O	S	N	S	Y	S	O	L	O	V	E	T	D	G	A	H
S	E	V	E	N	T	S	I	E	F	L	Z	B	C	E	A
I	J	O	Y	O	E	I	H	U	G	H	Y	G	Z	R	A
S	T	E	M	B	R	A	C	E	Z	B	T	S	X	P	T

Jerusalem	Lights	Jericho
Builders	Embrace	City
Trumpet	Elisha	Joshua
Walls	Son	Seven
Preach	Mouth	Love
Paul	Stretch	Joy
Midnight	Child	

Unscramble the words below

elsbs

inap

ithaf

nefoesrvisgs

neciepta

epeac

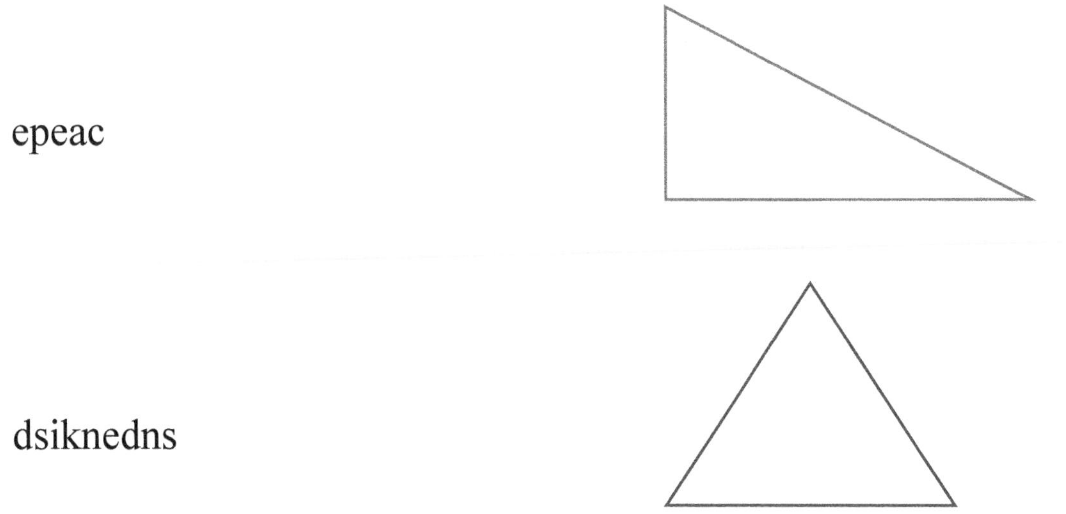

dsiknedns

Draw five healthy foods.

Answers to the puzzle and unscrambled words

S	R	N	U	T	R	I	T	I	O	N	G	J	K	Y	D
G	I	S	K	R	H	G	O	D	D	Z	T	O	T	I	W
S	W	G	L	F	T	B	R	O	E	P	E	Y	E	C	S
C	A	F	S	A	B	B	A	T	H	C	M	T	U	S	A
H	T	H	R	I	D	R	A	F	I	H	P	G	R	F	B
O	E	Z	F	P	K	E	C	F	S	T	E	R	A	C	A
O	R	O	E	X	E	R	C	I	S	E	R	O	N	I	A
L	G	E	L	J	E	R	B	D	M	E	A	W	R	T	L
S	I	G	S	U	N	D	I	A	L	G	N	T	Z	A	H
J	B	Y	T	T	D	M	C	F	E	T	C	P	F	P	A
U	P	J	E	S	U	S	W	A	S	H	E	E	R	T	P
D	T	S	U	N	L	I	G	H	T	W	T	Z	W	T	P
A	O	T	R	U	S	T	I	N	G	O	D	Q	O	R	Y
H	D	T	Z	R	S	W	T	Z	Q	H	Z	K	C	A	W
I	J	F	A	I	T	H	F	U	L	Q	Z	K	C	E	A
T	S	S	I	N	G	I	N	G	B	T	W	E	Q	H	X

Nutrition	Trust in God	Sun dial
Diet	Sabbath	Jesus wash
Exercise	Heart	Happy
Water	God	
Sunlight	Singing	Judah
Temperance	School	
Air	Faithful	

Puzzle

A	E	J	E	R	U	S	A	L	E	M	S	F	G	Y	T
M	C	U	F	I	S	S	O	F	E	I	S	L	L	E	W
B	V	P	Z	B	R	O	B	E	C	A	V	E	F	A	P
U	F	F	M	I	D	N	I	G	H	T	M	V	L	X	I
I	J	L	E	D	I	R	Y	F	I	G	B	L	K	T	P
L	O	M	O	U	T	H	F	H	R	V	S	K	T	A	L
D	S	E	A	A	T	M	R	R	I	B	T	Y	U	I	O
E	H	R	P	L	T	H	T	H	G	N	R	L	G	P	O
R	U	E	J	E	R	I	C	H	O	F	E	H	S	T	E
S	A	N	I	X	P	E	Q	R	T	M	T	P	T	S	L
T	L	T	R	U	M	P	E	T	L	S	C	K	X	H	I
S	E	A	D	T	V	F	D	K	X	Y	H	R	I	C	S
O	S	N	S	Y	S	O	L	O	V	E	T	D	G	A	H
S	E	V	E	N	T	S	I	E	F	L	Z	B	C	E	A
I	J	O	Y	O	E	I	H	U	G	H	Y	G	Z	R	A
S	T	E	M	B	R	A	C	E	Z	B	T	S	X	P	T

Jerusalem	Lights	Jericho
Builders	Embrace	City
Trumpet	Elisha	Joshua
Walls	Son	Seven
Preach	Mouth	Love
Paul	Stretch	Joy
Midnight	Child	

Unscramble

Bless

elsbs

Pain

inap

Faith

ithaf

Forgiveness

nefoesrvisgs

Patience

neciepta

Peace

epeac

Kindness

dsiknedns

www.ingramcontent.com/pod-product-compliance
Lightning Source LLC
LaVergne TN
LVHW071942210726
843527LV00042B/590